Riptide

ART AND STAINED GLASS

ART AND STAINED GLASS

CLAUDE LIPS

DOUBLEDAY & COMPANY, INC.
GARDEN CITY, NEW YORK

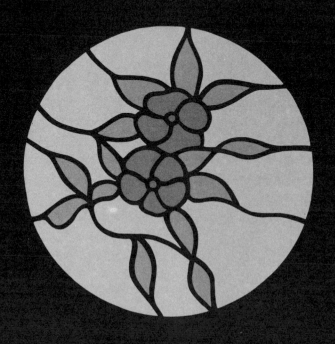

With thanks to Ellen and Gene Andes for help
in the preparation of the manuscript of this book,
to Gene Andes for the line drawings, and to Larry Songy
and Mike Smith for the photography.

ISBN: 0-385-08286-x
Library of Congress Catalog Card Number 72–92255

14259

This book is fondly dedicated to "The Old Man"
—Louis Dittrich, master art-glass mechanic, with whom I
served my apprenticeship

CONTENTS

ART AND STAINED GLASS

MATERIALS

Glass .

Any glass used for artistic purposes may be termed art glass. To the glass worker, however, art glass refers to the traditional art of construction of leaded glass panels with many individual pieces of colored glass assembled into a pleasing pattern, design, or picture. This is the type of work most people call "stained glass." As properly defined, stained glass is only that glass which has been painted with special pigments and kiln fired to fuse the pigments with the superficial layer of the glass. Today, stained glass is made by only a few of those glass workshops with an art-glass department. Most of you will be able to design and create beautiful panels, lamps, and decorative accessories using the tremendous variety of art glass available without need to stain your own glass. The equipment and supplies for staining glass are expensive, and the techniques are closely guarded secrets, even today, so if you wish to color your own glass, you must be prepared to spend a lot of money and time. Fortunately, there is such a wide variety of colors and textures of art glass available that it is usually unnecessary for the modern worker to stain his own glass.

Before you can intelligently decide on the glass to use in a particular project you must know something about the various types of glass suitable for use in art-glass construction.

The most common glass, *window glass,* is mass produced, flat-drawn sheet glass either $\frac{1}{16}$-inch thickness (single strength or SS glass) or $\frac{1}{8}$-inch thickness (double strength or DS glass). In the manufacture of this glass, the molten-glass mixture is drawn flat by machines and stretched to the desired size and thickness. The drawing process produces glass with minor irregularities in the surface, probably due to the uneven cooling and stretching of the semifluid glass sheet. These irregularities appear visually as slight, wavy distortions which are most noticeable when the glass is viewed at an acute angle. When window glass is used in small panes, as for a home window, this distortion is of no consequence, but when glass is used for large commercial windows the distortion is a problem, and other types of glass are preferred. Window glass is graded A or B according to quality—A is better, with type B being used most commonly for the home because of its lower cost. Window glass is occasionally used in leaded glass panels and type DSB is recommended.

In general, the thicker the glass, the stronger the glass. The larger the size of a single unsupported pane of glass, the stronger it must be and, thus, the thicker it must be. Although art-glass work usually involves relatively small pieces of glass, glass of ⅛-inch thickness is used because the lead channel is designed for glass of this thickness and because the panel with thick glass will be stronger than one made with thin glass.

There is also clear art glass available, usually ⅛-inch thick, some of which is "seeded." The glass contains small air bubbles that were added to the molten glass before drawing and appear in the final product as small elliptical bubbles or "seeds." This type of glass is specially made for use in art-glass work and is more expensive than window glass, but is generally preferred by workers for its greater beauty. Clear art glass is harder to cut than window glass, but with practice, you will be able to work with the harder glass, and I am sure you will find its better appearance ample reward for any difficulties in learning to work with it.

Crystal sheet is similar to window glass but thicker. Like window glass, it is flat-drawn sheet containing slight surface irregularities causing wavy distortions, which are more visible in the thicker glass. Since thick glass is used for large commercial windows in which any distortion is unacceptable, crystal sheet has largely been supplanted by plate glass.

Plate glass is flat-drawn sheet glass that has been ground and polished on both surfaces to produce a perfectly smooth glass of uniform thickness. Plate glass is nearly distortion free and is the glass most used for large windows or doors in the home or in commercial buildings. Plate glass is available in many thicknesses, ranging from ⅛ inch to 1 inch or better, with ¼ inch and ⅜ inch being the most commonly used sizes. There are many specialized types of plate glass available, such as tinted, heat absorbent, and tempered glass, but these are made for architectural applications and are little used in art glass. I occasionally use ⅛-inch plate instead of DS window glass, but for most jobs, the significantly higher cost is not justified. In addition, I use ¼-inch or ⅜-inch plate glass for construction or repairing of beveled glass panels. Most other applications of plate glass are in the realm of the general glazier.

Obscure glass is a general term for clear glass of any type that has been treated to make it translucent rather than transparent. This glass will admit light without permitting a person to see clearly through it. Such glass may be "frosted" by sandblasting, or it may be patterned by molding, chipping, or otherwise creating a distorting surface on one side. Intended for use in bathroom windows, office doors, shower stalls, and the like, obscure glass is not often used in art-glass work.

Etched glass is glass in which part of the glass has been removed by chemical or mechanical means from one surface of the glass. Etching is used to mark monograms, trademarks, letters, or figures on a pane of glass which may then be installed in a leaded panel or conventional window frame. Early workers etched glass with hydrofluoric acid, a particularly dangerous material, in a long tedious process involving the application of an acid resistant protective coating to the portion of the glass to be left unetched, timed exposure to the acid solution, removal and neutralization of the acid, and treatment of the glass to stabilize it and prevent further action of the acid. Modern glass workers etch glass by sandblasting it. After application of a protective tape to the glass surface, the design is cut out of the tape and the glass exposed to a powerful blast of compressed air containing abrasive grit of the appropriate type. Sandblasting is somewhat hazardous and requires fairly costly equipment and supplies, but it is the etching method preferred by most modern glass workshops. If you wish to use etched glass, you may be able to find a local company with the necessary equipment to do the work for you. Otherwise you will have to experiment with acid-etching glass, a technique not recommended for beginners. Glass may also be etched by grinding with special small abrasive wheels mounted on a bench grinder or in a hand-held grinder. Because the grinding wheels are round, the cut produced in the glass will have sloping sides, and this technique is generally not suited for etching flat pieces of glass. It is however, the preferred method for producing etched or "cut glass" tableware.

Art glass is presently being made by several companies

in this country and in Europe. The glass produced is for the most part exceptionally well made, so the art-glass worker has available a wide range of consistent permanent colors in glass of good quality and a variety of finishes. (See color photos.) When buying glass by a reputable manufacturer, you may expect that the color will remain unchanged with exposure to sun and the elements through several lifetimes. Art-glass work that fails to stand up with time fails usually through poor design or construction technique rather than deterioration of the glass. Unfortunately, the materials other than glass which you will use in art-glass work, are not as long lasting as the glass so we will necessarily have to emphasize the techniques of construction in our later sections. If you buy quality art glass, you will have the best product available and it will be up to you to learn to do the kind of quality work that fine art glass deserves.

The beginner should not be overwhelmed by the great variety of art glass being made today. As you will quickly learn, the art-glass worker does best to restrict his buying to two or three types he prefers to work with, buying other kinds only when needed for a particular job. But the only way you will learn which types of art glass you prefer is by working with as many types as possible, which will involve some expense on your part. As a general guide to your buying, here is a brief list of the more popular types with my comments on each.

Contemporary design in art glass tends toward the use of simple shapes of vivid color assembled into abstract or geometric patterns. The glass used in such designs is usually one of the translucent art glasses of which *German Antique* and *Blenko* art glass are the most beautiful.

German Antique glass is made in West Germany and is a relatively smooth glass of fairly uniform thickness specially treated during manufacture to contain small air bubbles and faults of a decorative nature. The air bubbles or "seeds" are present in great numbers in heavily seeded German Antique and in lesser numbers in the lightly seeded variety. Some lightly seeded German Antique glass has a brushed surface with a swirled and wavy pattern. There is a wide variety of colors available.

Blenko glass is, in my opinion, the finest of the art glasses. It is mouth blown in cylindrical shapes which are then opened and laid flat. The color is of uniform density throughout the glass, but the mouth blowing process produces a glass with greatly variable thickness which when viewed in a panel will have lighter and darker areas within it because of the difference in thickness. This glass is available in sheets that change gradually from clear to colored or that shade from one color into another. Blenko glass is easy to cut, and its exceptional beauty and vivid colors make it the glass preferred for use in panels of relatively simple design. The only problems with Blenko glass are its high cost and variable thickness. The thickness in a sheet of Blenko glass may vary from under ⅛ inch to over ¼ inch. Since most of the lead channel used in art-glass work is designed for glass of ⅛-inch thickness, the thick portions of sheets of Blenko glass must be avoided or discarded when cutting glass for a standard panel. It is possible to fit thick glass into ⅛-inch channel by splitting the lead, but this seriously weakens the lead and is most emphatically not recommended. Thick portions of Blenko glass not suited for standard panels can be used in small jobs by installing it in extra-wide channel or in lamps where the glass is held by clips rather than channel, as will be discussed later. I feel that the exceptional beauty of Blenko glass is sufficient justification for its use, despite the slightly higher cost and waste. In addition, Blenko glass has a soft surface, making it slightly easier to cut than some other types of art glass, such as German Antique.

Other art glass being made today comes in a variety of surface finishes. The commonly used surfaces are termed smooth, granite, ripple, and hammered. Hammered art glass is often termed "cathedral glass" and is the type most often used by the hobbyist.

Opalescent art glass is a semiopaque glass of a marbleized appearance most often seen in older church windows and in doors, transoms, and windows of older homes. It is currently not as popular as other types of art glass because it does not transmit as much light as the translucent types, but when properly used, opalescent glass looks fine in even the most modern designs. For best appearance opalescent glass should be where it will receive strong illumination. It is available in sheets with one or two colors predominating or in sheets in which many colors are present with the colors shading from one to the other. A beautiful glass which I hope will regain its former popularity.

Flashed glass is clear glass with one side colored only in the superficial layer. When this colored layer is etched or sandblasted away, the treated area will be clear or frosted against a colored background. This type of glass is available in only a few colors and is intended for use in signs or dedication panels in which a name, date, or monogram is to appear. The most common example of the use of this glass is the "EXIT" sign.

Glass may be colored in other ways than those mentioned above. Applying silver nitrate and kiln-firing glass produces an amber or yellow color in the glass. This technique is often used in stained-glass studios to complement or modify the effect of the staining.

Before the development of companies producing art glass and the means to safely transport art glass over long distances, glass used in building was locally produced by small companies, which in many cases produced a glass of inferior quality and which lacked the knowledge necessary for the manufacture of colored glass. In those days, the art of staining glass was practiced by only a few companies and stained glass was relatively more expensive than today. Lacking good quality art glass, early workers tried many substitutes. Much old colored glass was just painted with transparent or translucent enamel and baked at low temperature. Because the pigment never truly fused with the glass and because the enamel has a different expansion and contraction rate than the glass, in all cases the color has or will separate from the glass. Many old church windows have areas of cracked, faded, or peeling color for this reason. The use of enameled colored glass was discontinued long ago by reputable professional glass workers.

In recent years many transparent and translucent enamels have appeared on the market for use in "duplicating" the appearance of "stained glass." I know of none of these that will not eventually crack and peel off the glass. Unless the glass is properly kiln-fired after painting, the pigment will not fuse with the glass, and the color must eventually separate from the glass. In short, if you wish to work with colored art glass, buy colored art glass. The better appearance and durability of the glass will be worth the extra cost.

For the beginner who wishes to practice the techniques of art-glass construction, I recommend the use of hammered cathedral glass. This glass is the softest of the art glasses and is, therefore, easier to cut and easier on the cutting wheel. It is also less expensive than other art glasses, so that your mistakes will be less costly while the glass is attractive enough that the finished product will be worth any difficulties in learning. After you have mastered working with cathedral glass you can experiment with the other art glasses, but save opalescent glass for last as it is the hardest of the art glasses and requires some experience.

When buying art glass, you may experience some difficulty in locating a supplier, particularly if you are an amateur or are located in a small town. The amateur or hobbyist will usually not be able to afford to buy enough glass to qualify for wholesale prices or quantity discounts. Most glass manufacturers and suppliers cater only to the trade and are not able or willing to process and ship small orders, particularly mail orders. By checking the phone book you may be able to locate a retail outlet near you or find a supplier who will handle small mail orders. If you live in or near a city having a glass company with an art-glass department, it may be possible to buy scrap pieces or remainders of sheets of art glass. Most beginners, however, will have to rely on the limited selection of a hobby shop or art supply store. The prices at the latter type of supplier will necessarily be the highest, so you will be rewarded if you diligently search out other sources of supply.

Sometimes you will be able to get old glass from a church or other building that is being demolished or remodeled. Glass removed from old windows will have to be cleaned of weatherproofing cement before it can be reused, but often the savings in money is worth the trouble, particularly for the amateur. If you aren't getting the glass free, be sure to inspect all that you buy to be sure it isn't the enameled glass described earlier. You will not be able to reuse the lead from such windows, so when selecting the glass, leave the lead behind, especially when buying the glass by the pound. Many salvage companies are interested in reclaiming the lead only, and may let you have the glass for free if you leave the lead for them.

Be careful buying old windows in junk shops. The price is often inflated on the mistaken belief that old glass is more valuable than new. You will probably find that buying glass

Use over a door for this painting

Semicircular windows were often used over doors and windows. The rising sun pattern shown appeared in many variations.

from such places will be more expensive than buying new glass. Reputable antique dealers, on the other hand, often will have panels of exceptional merit, panels which in many cases have been restored by a competent art-glass worker. These panels are properly regarded as antique works of art and should not be purchased to be disassembled as a source of glass for your own projects.

Some old church windows may contain Tapestry glass, which is a colored art glass folded and formed during its manufacture to re-create the flowing folds of garments and robes. This glass is very rare and valuable and is no longer made today.

Old windows may also contain back-up pieces, which are additional layers of glass placed behind the main piece to modify its color or texture. The technique was used so the artist in charge of the window could obtain exactly the effect he wanted. I know of windows with as many as four layers of glass (three back-up pieces). The greater range of color available to the modern worker and the high labor cost in this technique make it largely unnecessary today.

Because I do a substantial amount of repair work, I keep quite a stock of antique and discontinued styles of glass, many inherited from my father. Unless you can get old glass for free, or at a bargain price, the beginner should pass it up and work with new glass.

Lead

The lead used to hold the glass in a leaded glass panel is specially made for that purpose. It is channeled to receive the edges of the glass, and when properly applied makes a secure weatherproof seal with the glass. The glass worker terms lead channel a "came."

Cames are available in many sizes and shapes, each type intended for a particular application. There are single channel (U-type) cames for use on the edges of a panel and double channel (I-type) cames for use wherever two pieces of glass abut. The center core of a came is termed the "heart," and the height of the heart is related to the thickness of the glass to be used, usually about ⅛ inch. The depth of the channel determines the amount which the lead overlaps the edge of the glass.

The "face" of the came is that part which is exposed when the panel is complete; it may be rounded, flat, or beaded ("milled").

Round, flat, and milled lead.

Section of lead channel.

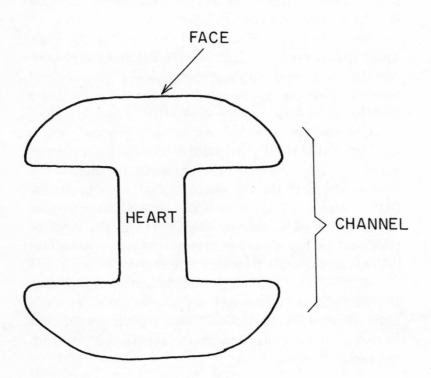

18

There are, fortunately, two types of came that will suffice for most work. The first type, Colonial Lead, is an I-type lead with a rounded, relatively narrow face that will bend around corners with a minimum of kinking. The shallow channel with its small overlap may not be sufficient to hide the beginner's irregular cut edges, however. Colonial lead is also available with a high heart for use by experienced art-glass workers when leading thick glass. National Lead Company's type BG Lead is a recommended Colonial Lead for general work.

A flat lead such as National Lead Company's No. 13 Flat Lead has a greater glass overlap, but the deeper channel causes kinking when the lead is bent into curves or corners without special precautions. If the flat lead is restricted to use in panels with only straight lines, it is the better lead for the beginner. Otherwise, you should use Colonial Lead.

Lead is priced by the pound, and the price per pound varies with the amount purchased. The number of cames in a given weight of lead will vary with the style of came: Flat lead, being thicker and heavier than Colonial Lead, will have fewer cames and less total length than the same weight of Colonial Lead.

The lead is shipped as flat strips or coils. In either case, the cames will have to be straightened and the channels opened before use. Kinks and bends in the cames are removed by stretching, using a lead vise to secure one end to the workbench and pulling stoutly on the other end with pliers. If you can't locate or improvise a lead vise, have a friend hold one end for you. Do not overstretch the lead. Pull only hard enough to remove the kinks and bends. Overstretching the lead weakens and narrows the channel. A six-foot came should be stretched no more than one inch.

After the lead has been straightened, it should be stored flat and wrapped tightly in brown paper to prevent oxidation of the lead. Oxidized lead has a dull gray color in contrast to the bright silvery color of new lead. Oxidized lead must be carefully scraped clean whenever it is to be soldered in order for a secure solder joint to be obtained. In a large panel with many solder joints, this task would seem endless, so prevent the oxidation by proper storage. Remove only enough lead for the job at hand and return the unused portion to storage.

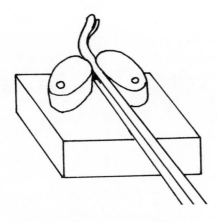

The lead vise holds one end of the lead strip when straightening lead.

Tools

There are few specialized tools required for art-glass work. Most of the tools you will use are commonly available and often already in the home workshop. You will need a lightweight carpenter's hammer, a ruler and a carpenter's square, household scissors, pencils, erasers, and a small box of 1¼-

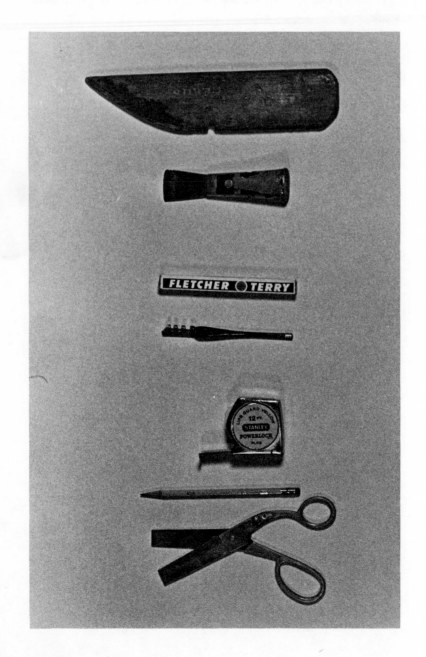

A minimum of tools is required by the beginner.

inch common nails. For making full-size layout and assembly diagrams you will need a roll of ordinary brown wrapping paper, compass, dividers, and a French curve template. You should also get some heavy pattern paper and carbon paper for transferring the layout drawing to the pattern paper.

The special tools you will need for cutting glass are a glass cutter—always termed a "wheel"—double-cutting pattern shears, plate pliers, and round-nosed pliers.

There are several types of glass-cutting wheels available each designed for a particular type of work. The wheel used for cutting art glass is not the same as the wheel sold in your local hardware store for cutting window glass. Art glass is much harder than window glass, and the wheel designed for use on art glass is made of harder steel than the ordinary wheel. You could use an ordinary wheel to cut art glass, but it would not do as good a job and would wear out quickly. Art-glass wheels are generally available only from a store or company stocking art-glass supplies, or directly from the manufacturer. The following table shows the different types of wheels available and the use of each.

Glass-cutting wheels—the number designations of the various wheels are from Somer and Maca Company's 1971 catalog.

USE	HANDLE TYPE	FLETCHER CO.	RED DEVIL CO.
Window glass	straight tip	01	024
Window glass	ball-tapping tip	02	023
Plate and heavy glass	straight tip	04	032
Plate and heavy glass	ball-tapping tip	05	
Opalescent and hard glass	straight tip	06	
Opalescent and hard glass	ball-tapping tip	07	
Safety glass, pattern, and shape cutting	straight tip	08	026
Safety glass, pattern, and shape cutting	ball-tapping tip	09	

The beginner should buy five or six wheels to keep on hand, as he will probably damage several wheels before mastering the technique of cutting glass. It is possible to sharpen a worn or damaged wheel, but very few people know how to do it properly. Although I sharpen my own wheels, I do not recommend that the beginner try to sharpen his. This diagram shows a steel wheel and its parts.

Diamond-tip glass cutters are available but they are expensive and difficult to control. They are of use to those men doing production work with extra-hard or plate glass, but are not often used by the art-glass worker.

Double-cutting pattern shears look like this. They are designed to make allowance for the thickness of the heart of the lead when the pattern pieces are cut directly from a full-size layout drawing. Although expensive, they are a real time saver. Their use and an inexpensive substitute are presented on page 30.

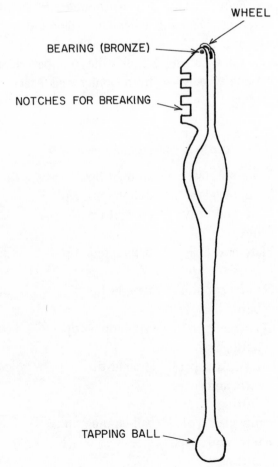

The steel wheel.

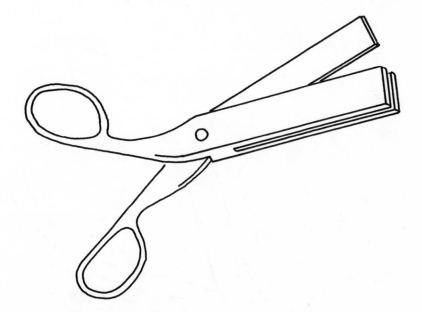

Pattern shears.

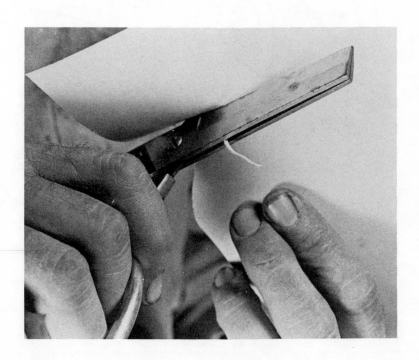

The pattern pieces are cut with pattern shears, which remove a narrow strip of paper by double cutting the pattern. In this way there is an allowance for the thickness of the heart of the lead came.

Round-nosed pliers are handy for trimming small pieces of glass from an irregular edge or for breaking small pieces of glass when attempting difficult cuts. I use these pliers instead of the breaking notches on the steel wheel.

Plate pliers are tongs with extra-wide gripping surfaces for applying breaking pressure over a wide area, as when cutting a strip from the edge of a large sheet of glass.

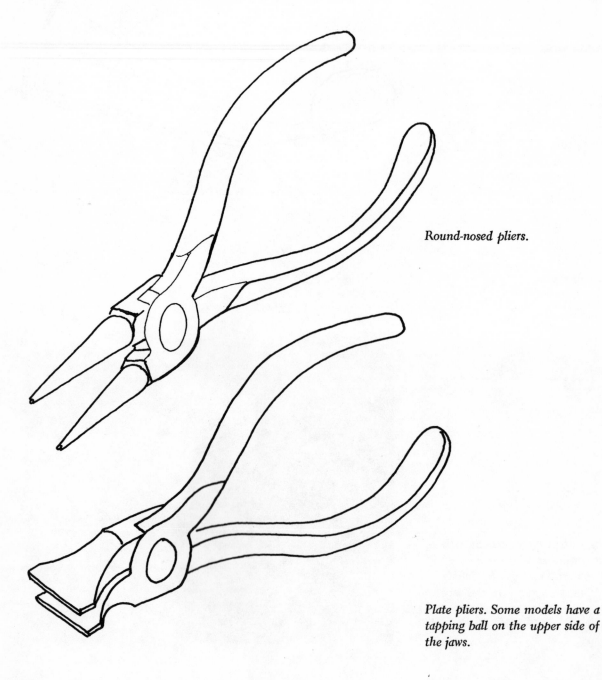

Round-nosed pliers.

Plate pliers. Some models have a tapping ball on the upper side of the jaws.

The tools required for working the lead are a lead cutter and a lead opener, both homemade. This diagram shows you how to make a lead cutter from a putty knife. The putty knife used should have a thin strong stiff blade. Do not use a putty knife with a flexible blade to make a lead cutter. The wide-bladed lead knives are made from a good quality wall scraper and are useful when trimming lead from an angle cut, as shown here.

Wide-bladed cutters are made from wall scrapers and are useful in making angle cuts.

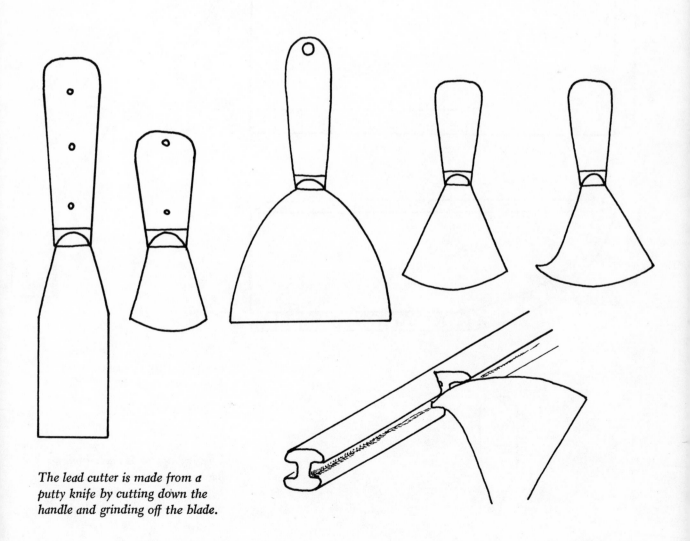

The lead cutter is made from a putty knife by cutting down the handle and grinding off the blade.

25

The lead opener is made from a piece of hardwood about 1×3×8 inches by sawing to shape and then carving and sanding the tip and lower edge as shown.

For sealing and weatherproofing the leaded panel, you will need two stiff scrub brushes and a bent-blade putty knife.

For soldering, use a large electric soldering iron. A large iron will not lose heat when soldering as quickly as a small one, so it will not be necessary to stop soldering to reheat the iron as much with a large iron. An iron with a half-inch diameter tip will be sufficient for most projects you may under-

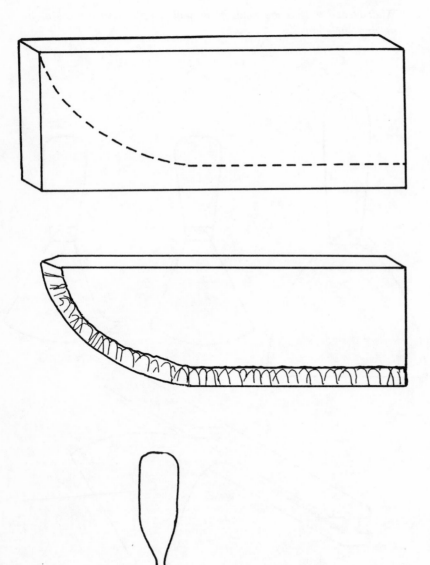

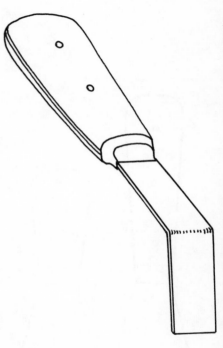

The bent-blade putty knife is available with 30 degree or 45 degree bend.

The lead opener is made from a hardwood piece 1×3×8 inches by sawing out the shape and whittling and sanding the edge.

take; I use a ⅞-inch diameter tip because so many of the panels I do are large and have many solder joints. Be sure the wiring in your workshop area is heavy enough for the iron you will use, and be sure to plug the iron directly into a wall outlet or a heavy duty extension cord, not a light extension cord. For soldering lead, the preferred flux is oleic acid. It is available from a chemical company and is used directly as supplied without addition of other agents. Apply the flux with a ½-inch paint brush.

I use $^{50}\!/_{50}$ wire solder (50 per cent tin and 50 per cent lead) although many persons prefer $^{60}\!/_{40}$ solder. In theory, $^{60}\!/_{40}$ solder should be stronger because of the higher tin content, but I have found that it makes little difference in practice. In a pinch, you could use acid-core solder, but it will not give as smooth or strong a joint as that made with oleic acid.

Panels made with heavy glass, as beveled plate, should be made with stronger channel than lead, although lead is sometimes used. I use zinc cames for assembling beveled glass panels. Zinc cames are cut with a fine-toothed metal-cutting circular saw and are notched by a special blade before joining by soldering with dilute muriatic acid as the flux. Zinc could be cut with a jeweler's saw and notched with a file in the home workshop.

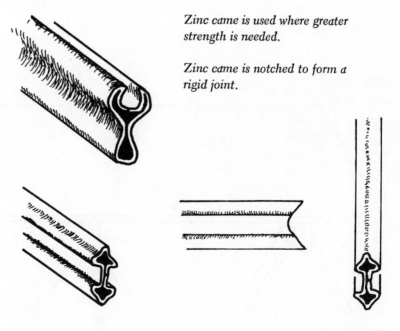

Zinc came is used where greater strength is needed.

Zinc came is notched to form a rigid joint.

WORK AREA

Art-glass work requires a relatively large amount of space as well as permanent storage areas for glass, tools, and supplies. Because it is necessary to make a full-size drawing of a panel before cutting the glass and assembling the panel, you will need a work surface large enough to accommodate the finished piece. In my shop I have two tables which are in constant use because there are many projects in various stages of completion at any given time. For the person who will be carrying a project through the various stages to completion before beginning another, a single table will suffice. A 4-×8-foot sheet of ½-inch or ¾-inch plywood on two sawhorses will provide enough room for your work and may be disassembled and stored when not in use. It should be about 28–30 inches high so you can work standing up. The minimum work area should be about 3×4 feet of unobstructed table space with good lighting, but a larger area will be much easier to work on. A simple bookshelf or cabinet with several drawers will provide storage for tools and lead. Glass should be stored vertically, ideally in simple racks like the one shown here. Never store glass of any kind in contact with concrete because the edge touching the concrete will become discolored and stained.

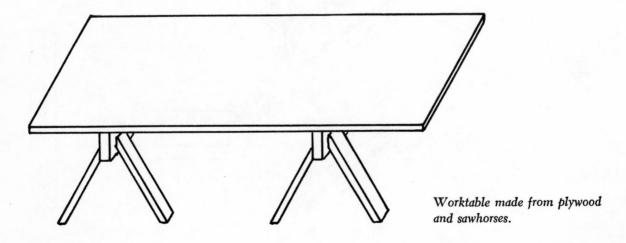

Worktable made from plywood and sawhorses.

The storage area should have a low humidity and a relatively constant temperature. Never store or carry glass or leaded panels flat.

When working it is a good idea to wear a heavy cloth apron, particularly when cutting glass or soldering to protect yourself from small glass fragments and acids. If you don't wear glasses, you may wish to wear safety glasses while learning to cut glass until you know how to control the breaking process. It is not necessary for an experienced worker to wear safety glasses however. Keep a small whisk broom or brush handy and sweep the worktable surface frequently when cutting glass. You will learn quickly to keep the table free of glass fragments. Never lean on the table with your hands or arms. A can of Band-Aids should be stored in a handy tool drawer.

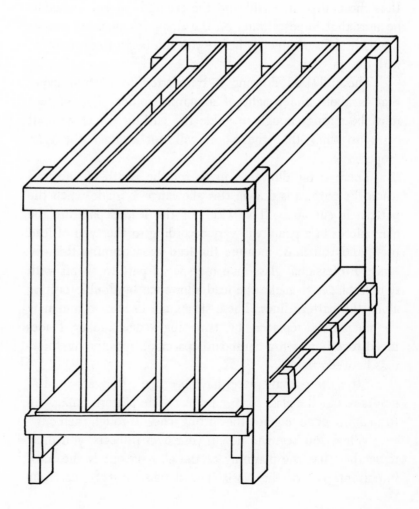

Glass storage area made of 2×4 lumber and plywood. The glass sheets are stored vertically and off the floor.

PATTERN DESIGN AND LAYOUT

In this section, we will present the steps in completing a small panel to illustrate how an art-glass worker approaches a specific assignment. It is not our intention that you copy this panel, although you may wish to do so, but rather that you will learn from this presentation the processes required in constructing your own designs. Later, in the chapter on Thoughts on Design, we will discuss the principles that guide the craftsman when he designs a glass panel. For now, we will pick up the process after the design has been drawn full size on drawing paper and the arrangement of glass and lead has been decided, because the beginner can appreciate the design limitations of glass work only after he has some knowledge of the tools and techniques used in construction of a panel. It is the craftsman's skill and the strength of the materials he uses that impose limits on the design. You must master the basic skills completely before you can begin to experiment with design.

The full-sized drawing is transferred to pattern paper that is about the weight of a manila folder. The pattern must be strong enough to guide the cutting wheel without being so thick that the wheel will not contact the glass properly.

There is no allowance made for the width of the lead when the pattern is drawn; this allowance is made when the pattern is cut apart. The width of the lead separating the glass pieces in a panel will vary according to the type of lead used, and you must measure the lead to determine this distance. Professional glass men use special pattern shears with double blades to make the lead allowance by double cutting along the pattern lines. These shears are expensive and may be adequately replaced by two single-edged razor blades taped together with a cardboard spacer of appropriate thickness between them.

After the pattern pieces have been cut, they are used as guides to cut the glass for the project. The pattern paper will form a firm edge to guide the cutting wheel through each cut.

When you begin to design your own projects, you must remember that the planning of the glass layout is the most important part of the work. The design must be carefully

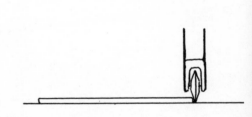

Pattern paper must be thick enough to properly guide the wheel, but not too thick.

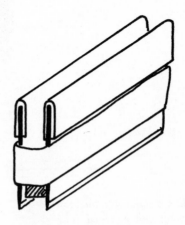

An improvised substitute for pattern shears.

made to conserve glass and reduce complex shapes into smaller, easily cut shapes. As you will see later, certain cuts are very tricky to make, and the project must be planned in accordance with your ability as a glass cutter. Inside curves and reversing curves are difficult to cut. Intersecting straight lines, as in a star, are even trickier. Even the experienced art-glass craftsman avoids these difficult cuts when possible.

As the pattern pieces are cut, place them on the master layout and number them. Notice the gaps left by the lead allowance. The letters on the pieces shown refer to the color of glass to be used.

The panel used for the example in this section was designed and executed in a limited series. Because several pieces were made, there were some tricks used to economize on materials and construction time. The rectangular pieces used as background and edging, for example, are all one inch wide. By using a standard width, I was able to strip one inch off the edge of several standard-sized sheets of glass making enough strips for several panels without wasting any glass. Notice also how the letters have been divided into small pieces of glass to simplify cutting and to reduce waste. The width of the letter pieces is also one inch, so glass used as edge in one panel may be used for letters in another. Remember that when you break a piece of glass attempting a difficult cut, that glass is wasted.

The second major aspect of panel design is the visual importance of the lead and other supporting metal. Since nearly all glass panels are back-lighted, the lead strips and other supports appear as stark, strong black lines crisscrossing the glass. These lines will be part of the design and may even dominate the final picture. As you gain experience in designing art glass, you will learn to use the lead in your planning.

Layout diagram for the panel LOVE.

Example

Small leaded glass panel with various types of translucent and opalescent art glass.

Door panel in opalescent art glass by the author.

Smooth-finish opalescent
glass in shades of green.

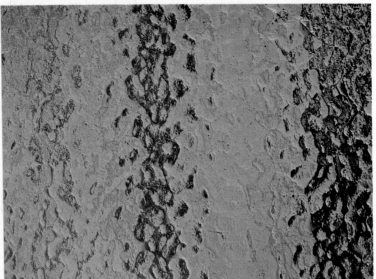

Green translucent art glass
with hammered finish.

Blue-green seeded German
Antique art glass (the stripes
are in the background curtain,
not in the glass).

Red-flashed glass with sand-blasted pattern.

Use for painting — needs masking fluid

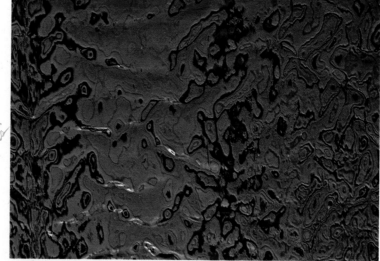

Brown translucent art glass with ripple finish.

Painting, use for

use for painting

Red opalescent art glass with granite finish surface.

Chapel Window Tharp-Sontheimer Funeral Home, New Orleans. A large panel in Blenko glass by the author for the Crasto Glass Company, New Orleans.

GLASS CUTTING

Straight Cuts

Glass cutting is actually a controlled fracture process. The cutting wheel rolls along the glass surface, scoring it and producing stress patterns within the glass which help to guide the break to be made. When you are cutting glass, the break should be made as soon after scoring as possible before the stress patterns dissipate and the cut becomes "cold." If you delay the breaking, the edge of the glass will not break cleanly and will have irregular jagged nubs remaining. In the extreme case, the glass will not break along the scored line, but in haphazard fashion.

Before every cut, the wheel is dipped in a solution of light oil (such as Three-in-One Oil) diluted 1 to 1 with turpentine. The oil and turpentine mixture cools and lubricates the wheel bearing, prolonging the life of the wheel.

When small pieces of glass are cut, a pattern is used to guide the wheel in scoring the smooth surface of the glass.

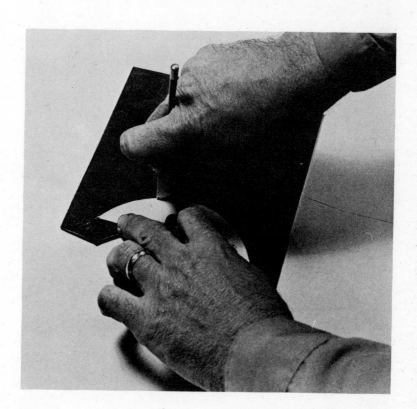

When scoring glass, the pattern guides the wheel through the cut.

use for painting

The glass is immediately fractured by breaking it in the hands, pushing upward in the line of the score mark while pushing down on the glass on each side of the cut. As breaking pressure is applied to the glass, you will see a fine fracture line develop just before the glass separates. In long straight cuts, this line, called a "run" may be started at one end and by continued pressure, caused to continue down the scored line in one rapid motion. In shorter cuts, the run may not be seen because the final breaking occurs almost instantaneously, but as you practice glass cutting you will soon recognize the run and learn to guide it through the cut by applying pressure at appropriate places and times. Control of the run is the basis of exact glass cutting.

For simple panels, most of the glass pieces will be small enough to break in the hands. The glass is held with the thumbs on the top, and the loosely curled fingers on the bottom of the glass, just a bit closer in toward the cut than the thumbs. The proper hand position is shown in the photographs and is illustrated in the diagram. The break is made by

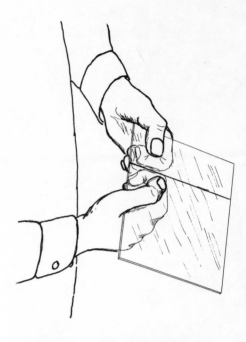

The position of the fingers when breaking glass with the hands.

With the break completed, notice that the hands have been rotated outward at the wrist.

pushing up with the fingers and down with the thumbs, rotating the hands outward at the wrists. Hold the glass slightly angled away from the body as shown so that any small glass fragments will fly away from you.

Occasionally a run may be started by tapping the glass with the steel ball on the handle of a wheel or on the plate pliers. Tap the glass upward from the under side in the line of the cut and then break it in usual fashion. Never tap down on the top of the glass. Breaking pressure is always applied to the side opposite the cut.

Long straight cuts may be broken over a ruler or table edge as shown. If the piece is narrow, use the plate pliers to apply breaking pressure starting at one edge of the cut, and once the run is started, advance the pliers until the run is complete and the strip will separate. If the piece is over three inches wide, make the break by applying pressure with the hands.

Stripping, or cutting straight pieces, is the best practice for the beginner. Lay the glass to be cut on the smooth clean surface of your worktable and, using a ruler or pattern piece as a guide, make the score mark on the top surface of the glass. Press down firmly on the wheel and make the cut in a single motion, starting and stopping just short of the edges. Do not run a wheel over an edge or it will notch and be ruined.

It is not necessary to make the cut rapidly, but neither should it be made very slowly. The important thing to learn is control of the wheel.

Immediately after scoring the glass, finish the cut by breaking the glass as described above. Whenever possible, make a single cut at a time. If the cut has been made properly, the glass will break easily along the line you have scored. The break will be straight and the edges clean where the glass was scored, and the break will go off at a diagonal from the ends of the mark.

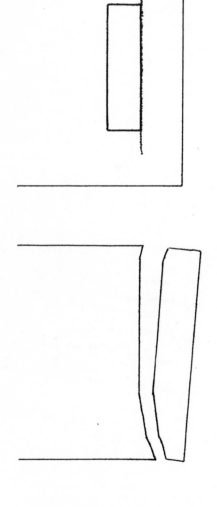

Straight cuts are easiest for beginners.

Breaking a strip of glass over a ruler or table edge.

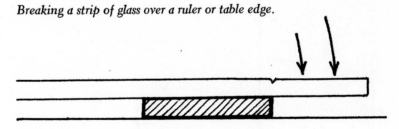

Sometimes a wheel will skip when scoring the glass. Skipping is usually due to a defective wheel with a notched or irregular edge or to a wheel that does not turn smoothly. The beginner may experience skipping due to uneven pressure on the wheel during the cut. Whatever the cause, a skip in the cut is a serious mishap and will ruin the subsequent break. If you have a skip in your score mark, the pattern of the skip may tell you the cause. Check the wheel edge carefully for notches, and see that the wheel rotates freely when pressure is applied. If the wheel is in good shape, you probably need more practice in cutting.

Never retrace a cut with the wheel. Because the wheel has made a tiny trough in the glass like the groove in a record, the wheel cannot exactly retrace the trough, and will ride up on the side and notch on the sharp edge of the trough. Not even an expert can exactly retrace a cut. If a skip has occurred at the beginning or end of a cut, you may complete the cut by starting the wheel just past the start of the skip and moving it toward the end of the cut. With experience, a cutter may fill in a skip by starting and ending the second cut within the skipped part of the line. See diagram.

A notched wheel must be discarded. If the beginner has trouble with skipping, he is advised to determine the cause, discard the glass with the skip, and cut a new piece of glass with a new wheel if necessary.

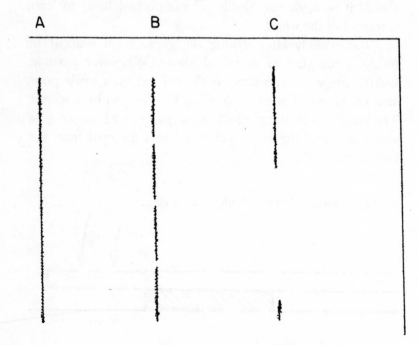

A   B   C

Defective cuts:
 a. Good cut
 b. Notched wheel
 c. Wheel stuck (bearing frozen), pressure too great or small

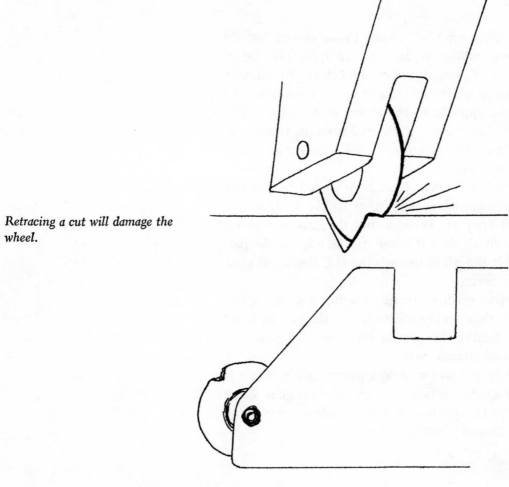

Retracing a cut will damage the wheel.

Filling in a skip.

Curved Cuts

There are three types of curves: inside curves, outside curves, and combinations of the two. All types may be of constant radius or of changing radius (French curve). An outside curve is one in which the glass to be removed is on the side of the curve opposite to the center of the curve. The waste glass on an inside curve is removed from the side of the curve toward the center. In general, outside curves are easier to cut than inside curves.

Once control of the wheel has been gained by practice with straight cuts, cutting outside curves will be fairly simple if you have a good pattern. When scoring the glass, start above the pattern and finish the cut below it. The edge of the pattern should guide the wheel through the cut. Break the glass in your hands as before.

When cutting small or sharply curving outside curves, you may use the third and fourth fingers of the cutting hand as a center of rotation by placing them on the glass and swinging the wheel around them.

Inside curves are also cut using a pattern guide, but it is necessary to use special caution when breaking the glass. Glass tends to break in straight lines and this tendency may cause the ends of the desired piece to fracture.

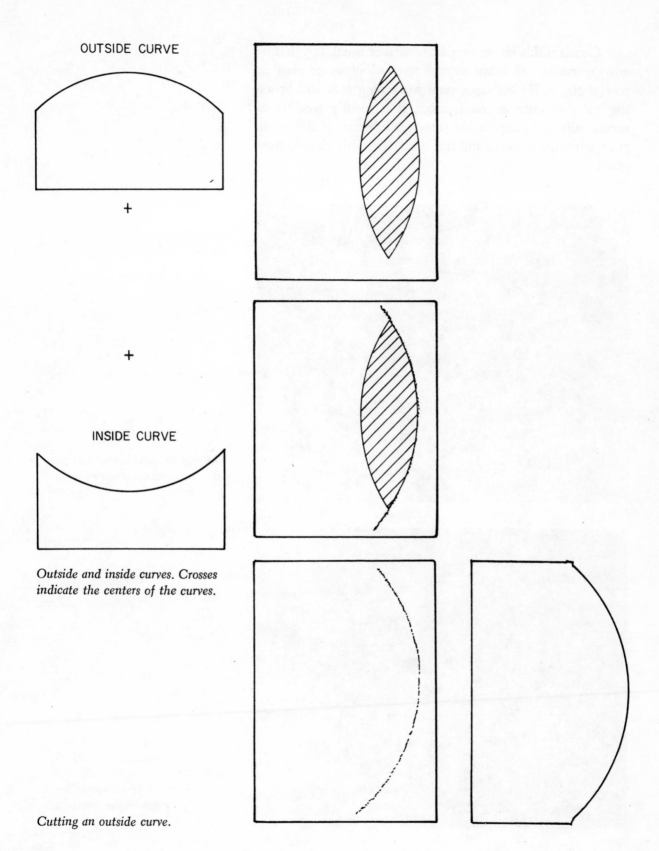

OUTSIDE CURVE

+

+

INSIDE CURVE

Outside and inside curves. Crosses indicate the centers of the curves.

Cutting an outside curve.

39

Gentle inside curves may be broken as usual, but sharply curving pieces will often require removal of waste glass in several stages. By making several weakening cuts and breaking out the waste in small pieces, it is usually possible to successfully cut sharp inside curves. Nibble away the waste glass with the notches on the wheel or with round-nosed pliers.

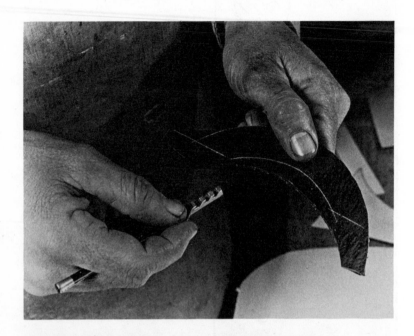

Cutting an inside curve. The score line has been made with the pattern.

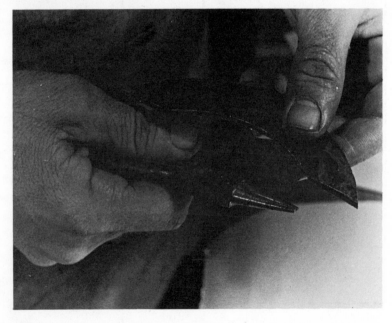

The nubs remaining after the curve is rough cut are removed with the round-nosed pliers. Grip the nub with the tip of the pliers and break it off with a twisting or rotating motion as shown.

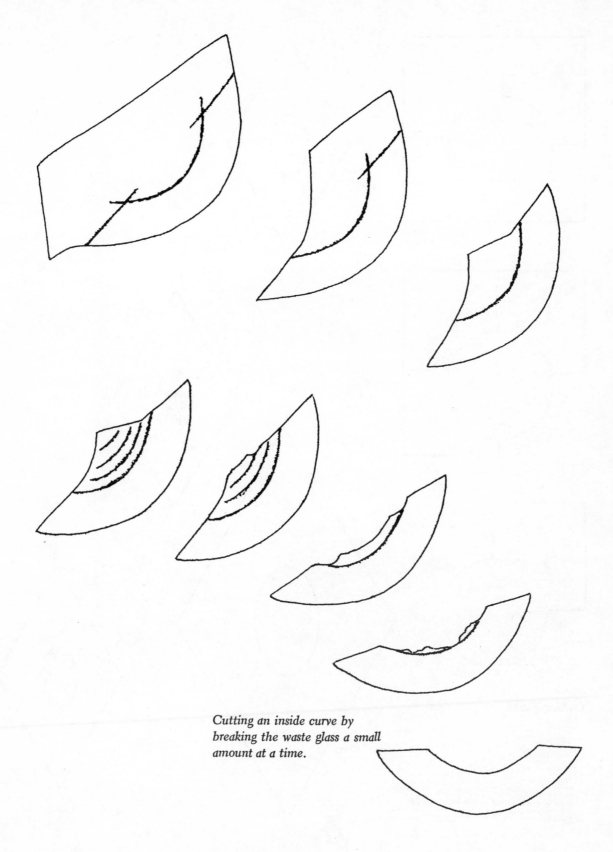

*Cutting an inside curve by
breaking the waste glass a small
amount at a time.*

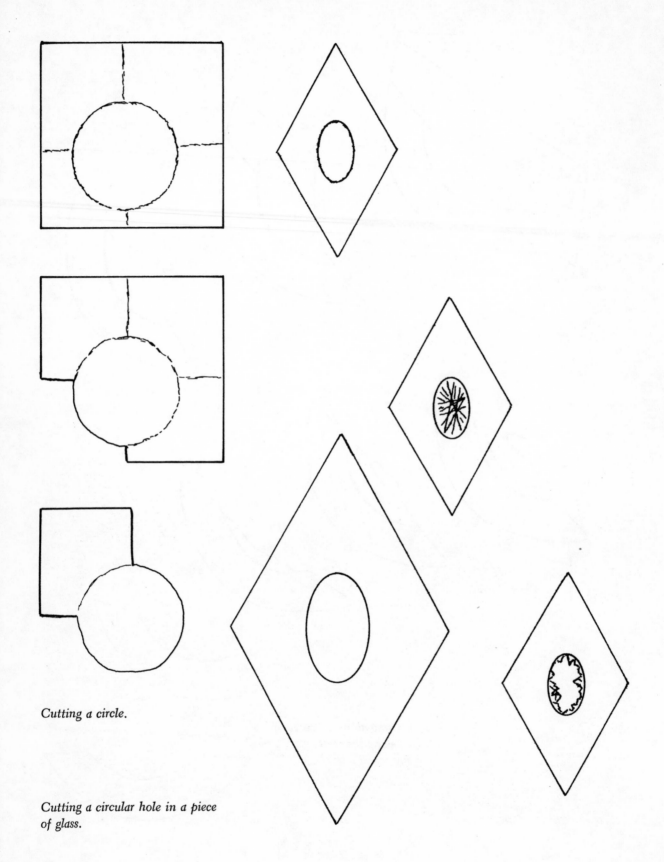

Cutting a circle.

Cutting a circular hole in a piece
of glass.

Circles are closed curves. A circular piece of glass is a closed outside curve. A pane of glass with a circular hole in it is a closed inside curve. The closed outside curve is usually cut in one pass with the wheel, and the surrounding glass broken away in several stages.

Cutting a circular hole in a piece of glass is difficult for the beginner. One way is to use weakening cuts.

After completing a cut, inspect the edge for irregularities and small nubs projecting from it. In order for the glass to fit properly into the lead channel, projections larger than ⅟₆₄ inch must be removed. Use your round-nosed pliers to gently trim the nubs off the edge. Use a rolling motion and break off a tiny piece at a time. At first, you will have a lot of trouble with flanges and nubs on the edges of the glass, but with practice you will learn to break the glass soon after scoring it and the irregularities will decrease.

As you cut the pieces for the panel, lay them on the original drawing as shown in the photographs and place the pattern pieces aside for future use. Later, drawings and pattern pieces may be folded and stored in manila envelopes if you wish to keep them on file.

As the pieces of glass are cut place them on the master drawing to avoid omission or duplication of a piece.

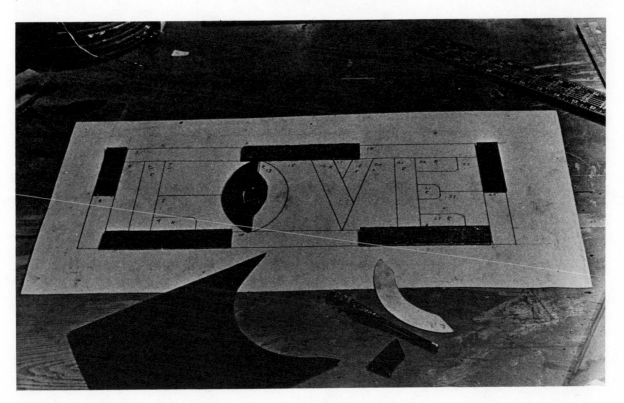

LEADING

Before lead is used, the channels must be opened and smoothed to receive the glass.

A lead opener is easily made, as described in the chapter on Materials. Lubricate the tip and curved edge with oleic acid, which is also the flux for soldering. If the opener is lubricated with oil, the oil will interfere with soldering. Open the channel by introducing the tip of the opener into the channel and sliding it along the channel. The lead for a panel is cut as you need it, working over the layout diagram.

When cutting lead always remember two things: Make the cut with a gentle rocking motion to avoid deforming the lead; allow for the overlap of the channel onto the glass when making corners.

Cut lead with a lead knife. I use a knife made from a putty knife. The blade should be as thin as possible throughout its length, without being too flexible. The curve of the cutting edge allows the knife to be gently rocked as the cut is made, decreasing the force required to cut the lead. If the

The lead opener opens and smooths the channel to better receive the glass.

Remember to allow for the overlap of the lead onto the glass when making a joint.

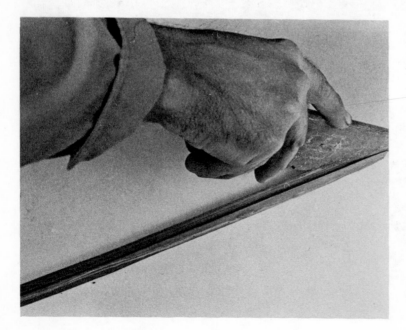

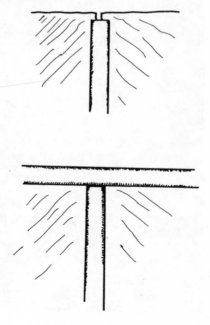

channel should be bent during the cutting, open it with the lead opener.

Once you have practiced cutting on a few scraps of lead, it is best to learn the process of leading a panel by practice. The diagram shows the basic types of joints you can use in assembling a panel. Usually only two of these are used in a panel and will be mastered with practice.

A panel is assembled directly on the full-size layout drawing. The panel must be assembled in a logical order, beginning at the lower left-hand corner and proceeding to the right and upward. It is possible to install the glass pieces in such a way that one area may become "boxed-in." Since the glass must be slid into the lead channel, a glass cannot be installed into an area surrounded by lead. This is the difference between

Basic joints used in leaded panels. Simple butt joint (Colonial Lead), tucked butt joint (flat lead), miter joint (corner).

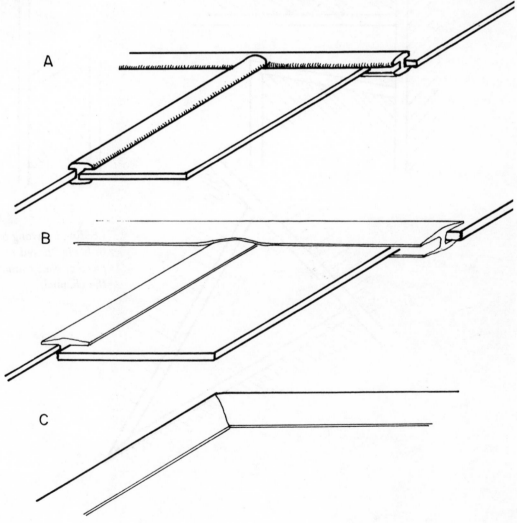

A

B

C

45

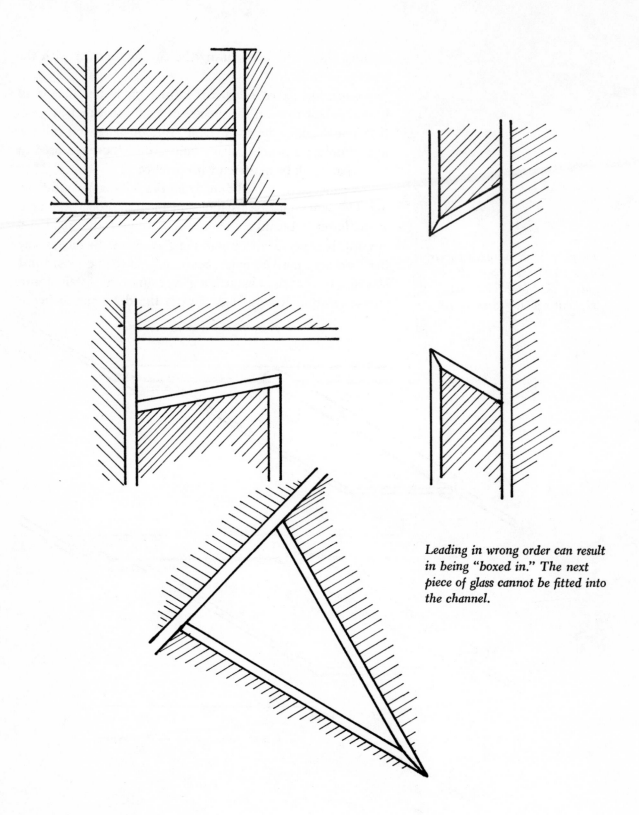

Leading in wrong order can result in being "boxed in." The next piece of glass cannot be fitted into the channel.

putting together a jigsaw puzzle and a glass panel. Here are some of the many possible cases where this may occur. When you are boxed in, the only cure is disassembly of the panel and reconstruction in proper order.

Mount the pattern on the worktable and nail two wooden strips along the left and lower edges. The first lead strips are cut to size and laid along the left side and lower edge. Join these strips at the corner in a mitered or a simple butt joint. Place the left-hand corner piece of glass in the channels of the lead pieces and tap gently with the handle of

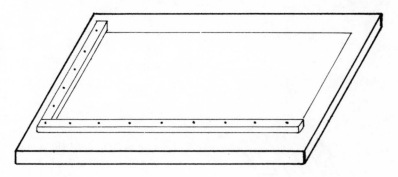

The leading table with wood strips nailed over the assembly diagram.

As you work, seat the glass well into the channel by tapping gently with the handle of the lead cutter.

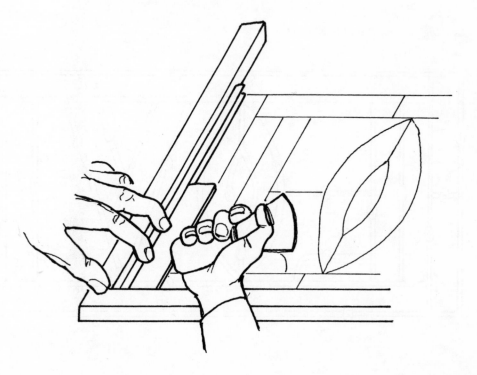

the lead knife or a small block of wood to seat the glass all the way into the channel. Cut and place lead along its upper side and similarly install the piece of glass above it. Cut a piece of lead to complete the right-hand edges of both pieces of glass and install it. This illustration shows the order in which the lead pieces are installed in the sample "LOVE" panel. No matter what type of panel you are leading, you should always keep the growing panel tightly clamped together by holding the free edge with small common nails

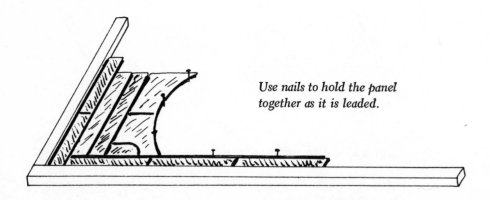

Use nails to hold the panel together as it is leaded.

Leading plan for the LOVE panel.

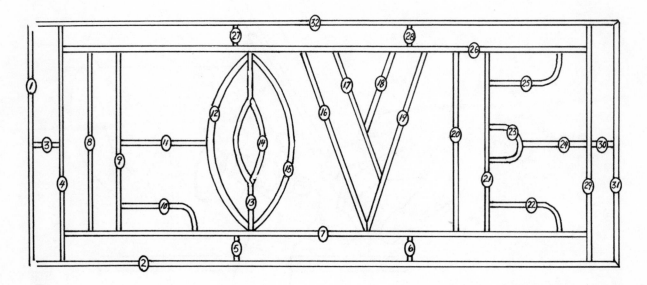

driven lightly into the table with a light hammer or the handle of the lead knife. These nails will prevent the glass from loosening as you cut the next strip of lead.

When leading curves and irregular edges, bend the lead in your hands. It is not possible to bend the last ½ to 1 inch of a strip of lead, so cut a piece longer than you will need, bend it, and then trim it to proper length. The steps in bending curves and circles and fitting the lead at the edges of a curved piece are shown in the photographs on page 51.

When leading a curved piece bend the lead in your hands until it fits the piece. As the lead is gently bent, the thumbs are slid along the inner side to prevent kinking the lead.

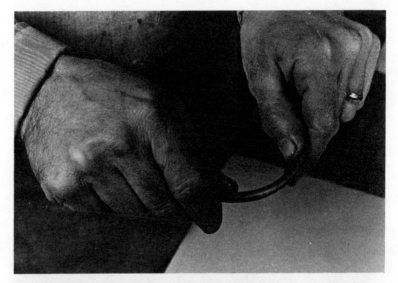

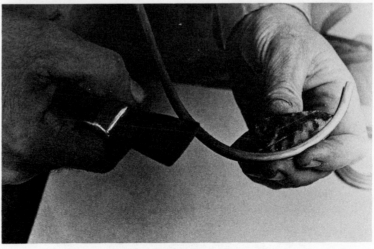

Bend the lead until the glass fits to it snugly.

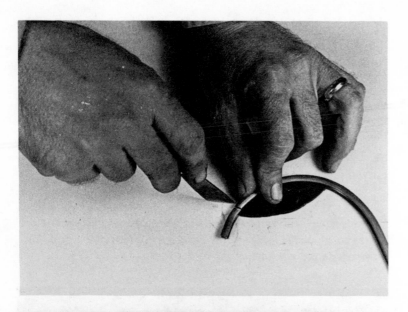

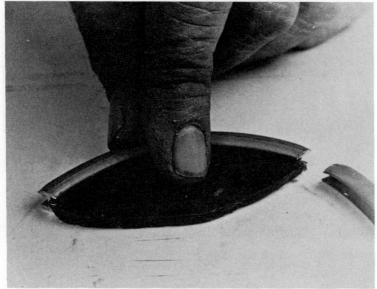

Mark and cut the lead after it has been bent being sure to make allowance for the overlap of the channel of the adjacent piece.

Leading a circle. The lead is bent in the hands and the joint marked and cut as shown.

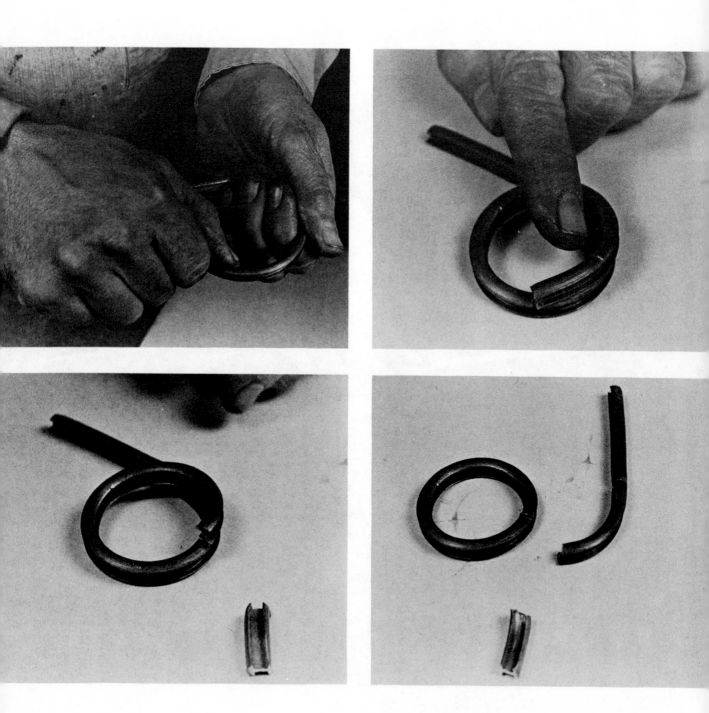

When leading a panel mark the lead directly on the growing panel as shown. Mark it with a small brad or with your thumbnail.

Only through practice will you develop the skill of rapid correct assembly of leaded panels. In general, you should let vertical lines "run through," that is, extend from top to bottom of the panel to increase strength. Otherwise, the choice of where to make a joint or cut a lead may be determined by considerations of beauty or by the length of the scrap pieces lying by your hand. As you gain experience, you will learn to minimize waste of lead by using your cut offs and short pieces whenever possible to avoid cutting into a new strip of lead.

The photographs illustrate the leading of a different panel in which there are only straight lines, the best type of panel for a beginner to attempt. The lead used in the panel shown is flat lead and it is joined in a "tucked" joint. A tucked joint is one in which the face of one lead slides under the face of the other lead. (See diagram on page 45.) The lead which will be on top is raised slightly with the lead knife to receive the other lead. Flat lead is always joined in a tucked joint, but Colonial Lead is joined in a simple butt joint.

When you work with glass of variable thickness, such as Blenko glass, you may have to open the channel slightly with the lead knife to accommodate the thicker portions of the glass. Always be sure that each piece of glass is well seated into the lead before proceeding to the next piece. Glass which is incompletely seated in the channel may separate from the channel or be incompletely sealed by the weatherproofing cement.

The edge of a panel under construction. Note the difference in thickness of the two pieces of glass (Blenko) and the allowance made for overlap of the adjacent channel.

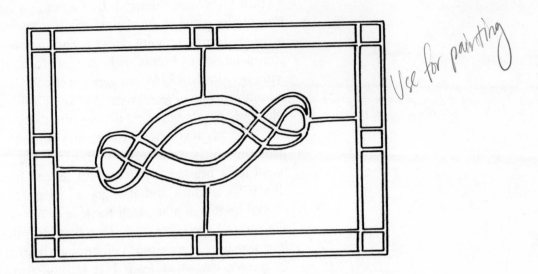

Use for painting

Glass fire screen showing the glass panel and the separate metal frame. For best appearance, use a clear glass in light colors for the center part of the panel.

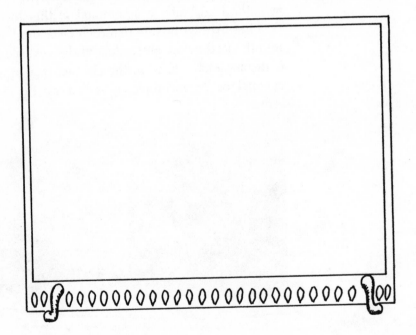

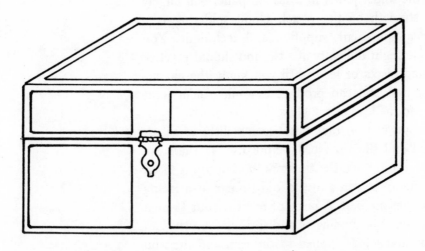

Small glass box. This can be made with U-channel lead soldered together at the corners, or with right-angle corner zinc channel (see insert). Hinges and latches are readily available at shops with decoupage supplies and may be soldered directly to the lead.

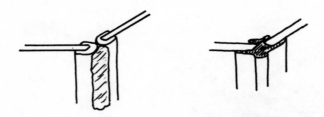

SOLDERING

The quality of the solder joints in a leaded panel will largely determine the strength of the panel. Good soldering is a matter of proper equipment, supplies, and technique. You must expect some slight difficulty at first, and should practice soldering on scrap pieces of lead until you know the characteristics of your iron and can produce a sound solder joint without damage to the lead or the glass.

A new iron or an iron that has become dirty or rough must be cleaned and the tip faced before use. If there are nicks or burrs on the tip, file the tip smooth. The tip is faced with a thin coating of solder. I use an old tin can as a facing surface—sardine cans are best. A piece of rosin (about ¼-inch diameter) is crumbled in the fingers and sprinkled on the can top, the hot iron and solder applied to the can, and the iron moved across the surface in a circular or figure-of-eight motion until both faces of the tip are covered by a smooth glistening layer of solder. Excess solder is removed by quickly wiping the iron with a piece of heavy duck or canvas cloth, and the iron is ready for use.

A dirty soldering iron tip should be cleaned and resurfaced.

Facing the soldering iron tip on a tin can with rosin and solder (or rosin-core solder). A tuna can is shown, but a sardine can is better shaped for the figure-of-eight motion used.

The usual electric soldering iron has a heating element that is on whenever the cord is plugged in. If left plugged in too long, the iron will become too hot, so it is necessary to regulate the heat by plugging and unplugging the iron as required. The iron should be hot enough to quickly melt the solder and to heat the lead to a temperature high enough to permit the solder to join with it, but it should not be so hot that it melts or burns the lead. Until you learn to judge the heat of the iron by looking at it, it is a good idea to test the iron on a piece of scrap lead before beginning to solder. After the iron has reached the proper temperature for soldering it is usually unplugged while the panel is soldered to prevent excessive heating. When soldering extra-heavy lead or assembling a very large panel, I will leave the iron plugged in, but I don't recommend this for the beginner. Since the iron loses heat each time a solder joint is made, the iron will gradually cool as you use it. The bigger the tip of the iron, the slower it will cool off, which is why I recommend the use of a large iron. While the iron is heating to operating temperature, I prepare flat lame for soldering by smoothing the tucked lead joints by tapping with the handle of the lead knife. Then apply oleic acid flux to all the solder joints. Brush the flux on with a small paint brush and be sure to use enough. But do not use excess flux as it dries slowly and will interfere with weatherproofing the panel.

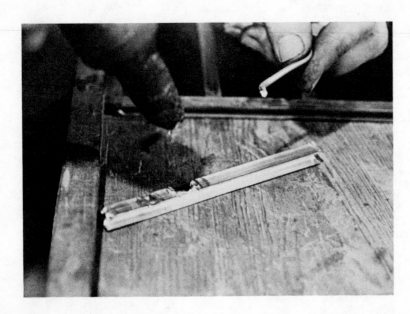

A soldering iron that is too hot will melt the lead. Remember that the melting point of the lead is only slightly higher than the melting point of the solder.

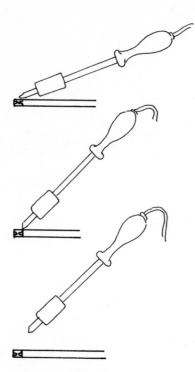

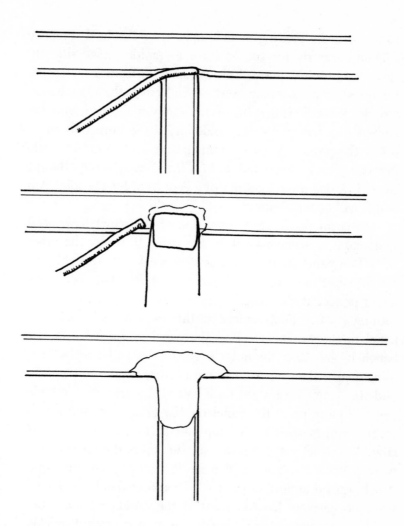

The soldering iron is lifted from a solder joint in a two-step motion: the handle is lifted first and then the tip.

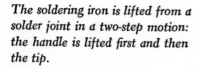

Solder is held over the fluxed joint. The hot iron is applied to the solder, melting it and heating the lead so that the solder flows smoothly over and into the joint.

Uncoil about two feet of wire solder and place it on the worktable. Test the iron on a small piece of solder to see that it is at the proper temperature, and you are ready to begin.

Hold the solder in your left hand and place about ¼ inch of it across the joint to be soldered. Place the iron on top of the solder and as it melts move the iron back and forth across the joint in a smooth motion so that the lead is also heated and the solder will flow into the seam between the two pieces of lead. After the joint is made, the iron is lifted from the lead in the motion shown in the diagram so that it will leave no mark on the solder or the lead. In a few seconds the solder will be hardened. At no time in the soldering process is pressure applied with the iron. The iron is held loosely so that the weight of the iron does the work. Pressure on the iron is likely to cause melting or deformation of the lead. Practice will be necessary for you to learn to rapidly make smooth, even, sound solder joints. You will have to learn some speed, for the slow worker may overheat and crack the glass beside a solder joint. This diagram shows some of the problems beginners may have with their soldering. If the iron cools off to below the proper operating temperature while you are working, you must replug it and wait for it to heat. Do not attempt to get just one more joint out of a cool iron, for the joint you do get will be a bad one.

After all the joints on one side of the panel have been soldered, it is necessary to turn the panel to solder the other side. The panel in this stage is very weak and unstable, so extreme care must be used when turning it. Many beginners lose a project at this stage. There is only one safe method of turning a panel. First, remove all the wood strips holding the panel to the workbench. Pull the panel to the edge of the bench by handling the outer edges of the panel or by handling the panel only in areas where a vertical lead runs through. Slide the panel toward you until half of it overhangs the table edge. Rapidly pivot the panel on the table edge until it is vertical and grasp it by the top and bottom or the sides. If large, the panel may be rested on the knees during this maneuver. Raise the panel and place it vertically on the workbench, turn it around so the back (unsoldered side) is facing you, and lower it down in front of the workbench until the middle rests against the table edge. Rotate it upward quickly and slide it back onto the work surface. Solder the second side exactly as the first and leave the panel in place on the workbench for cementing.

Good and bad solder joints:
  a. good solder joint
  b. iron too cool (lead not heated)
  c. not enough flux (solder does not flow)
  d. iron too hot (lead burned)

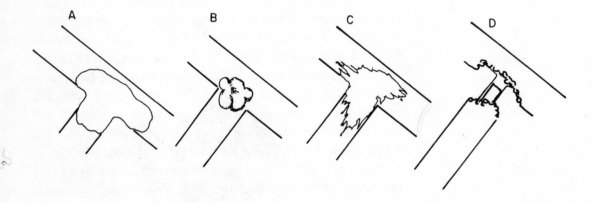

A   B   C   D

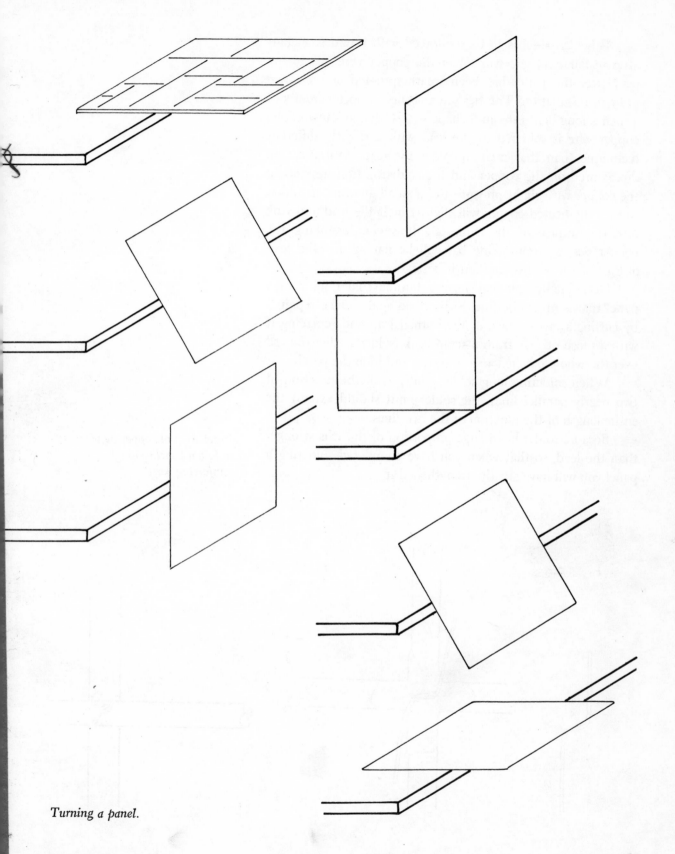

Turning a panel.

When a panel is to be reinforced with round steel bars after installation, you will solder the copper wire ties to the lead after the panel has been weatherproofed and cleaned prior to installation. The ties are 12-gauge copper wire about 4 inches long bent into an S shape with pliers, as shown. The copper wire is soldered to the lead with a slightly different technique than that used to solder the lead. Muriatic acid flux is used on the copper and the soldering iron applied to the copper with slight pressure and a small amount of solder, so that the heated copper will slightly melt the lead and sink into the surface of the came. By thus countersinking the copper ties, the reinforcing bar will lie flat against the lead of the window and strengthen it better.

Occasionally you may have a burned solder joint in a panel that is otherwise fine. Such a bad spot can be repaired by cutting away the face of the burned lead and replacing it with a piece of face from a scrap lead. Solder is then flowed over the whole patched area to secure and hide the patch.

When soldering long solder joints, as in the junction of two nearly parallel lines, the solder joint should extend the entire length of the junction of the two lines.

Because solder has a large proportion of tin, it is stronger than the lead, so that when you have completed soldering a panel you will have greatly strengthened it.

Installation of copper tie wires to fasten panel to rough reinforcing bars.

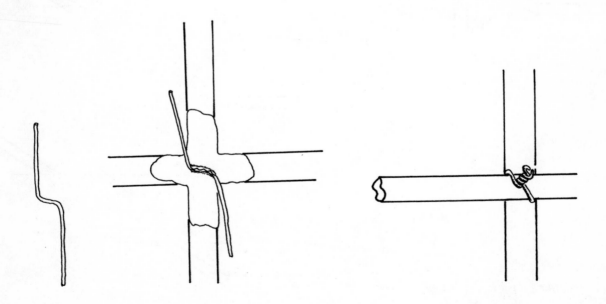

Long joints should be soldered through their entire length.

Repairing a burned solder joint by replacing the face of the lead.

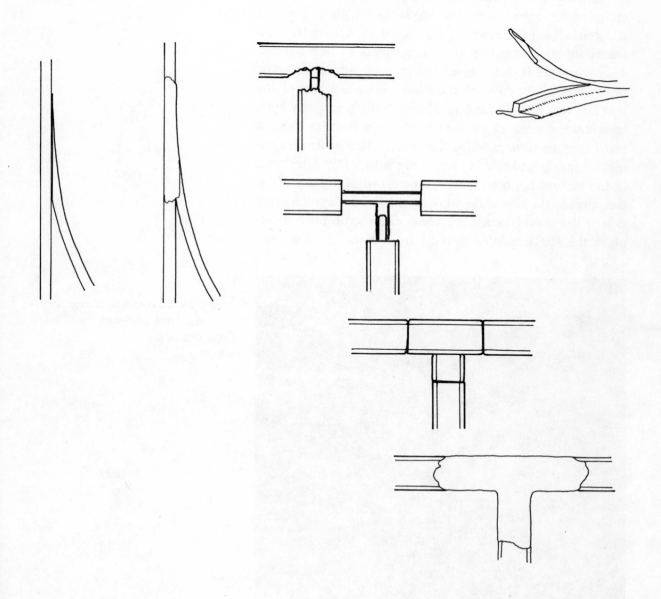

SEALING

As you move the soldered panel on your workbench you will probably notice that the glass is loose in the channel, in many cases loose enough to rattle. A panel intended for use in a door or window cannot be left this way, for in time the movement of the glass will increase and eventually the glass will work free of the lead. In addition, leaded glass left in this condition will leak in the rain and admit air between the glass and the lead.

Sealing of the panel is done after soldering and before crimping the edges of the lead to clamp the glass. The best sealer is a cement made by diluting steel sash putty with linseed oil and turpentine to the consistency of heavy cream. This thin paste is then applied to the panel with a stiff scrub brush, taking care to work the sealer under the face of the lead and well into the corners. Then use the bent putty knife to crimp the edges of the lead firmly onto the glass. Excess sealer is removed by covering the panel with a generous coating of sawdust and rubbing vigorously with a rag. After most of the cement has been removed, the sawdust is brushed off the panel to the side of the work area, for use when the other side of the panel is cemented. Use a clean scrub brush to remove the last remaining sawdust from along the lead and

Apply weather-sealing cement with a scrub brush and work it well into the channels.

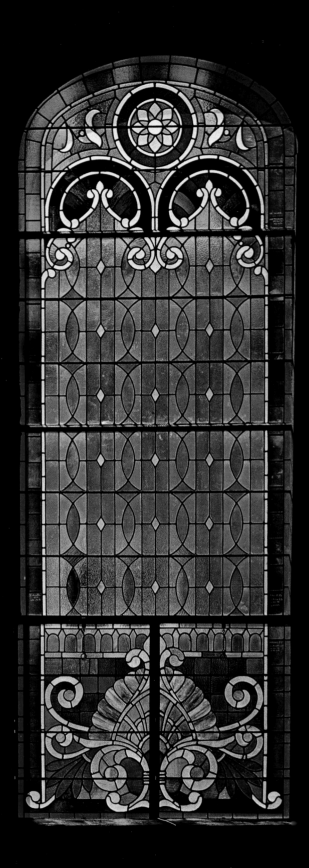

Use
for
painting

Window in St. Louis Cathedral,
New Orleans.

Hanging lamp of art glass. In this piece, copper or zinc channel is used for strength, rather than lead came which would deform with the weight of the lamp. The glass has been molded to shape by kiln firing.

Lamp shade of kiln-molded Blenko glass by the author and Louis Dittrich.

Use for painting

Entryway with door, side lights, and overhead panel of beveled glass in the traditional La Louisianne *pattern. Executed by the author for the Henry Lips Glass Company.*

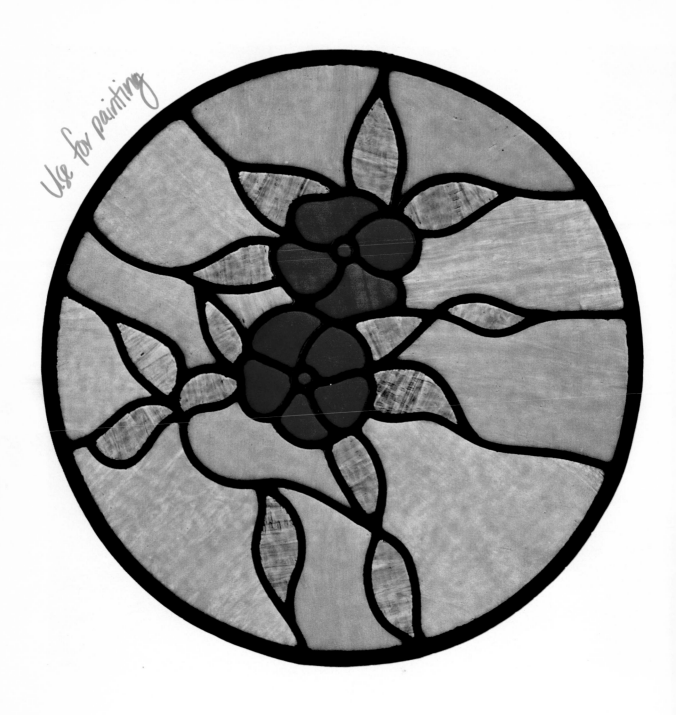

Use for painting

Circular leaded glass panel in three colors of opalescent art glass. This piece is designed to be hung as shown or incorporated into a larger panel.

After the cement has been applied, crimp the edges of the lead by sliding a bent blade putty knife along the edges of the channel.

Remove excess cement by sprinkling on sawdust, which will soak up the cement and oil. Remove the sawdust with a rag and scrub brush.

from the corners. Sprinkle Spanish Whitening over the entire panel and rub the glass and the lead with a clean rag. The Spanish Whitening dries up the last remaining cement and removes the oil from the glass. Both Spanish Whitening and sash putty should be available from a local paint or hardware store.

Turn the panel and repeat the process on the other side. After sealing, the panel should be stored for several days before installation. The cement requires at least twenty-four hours to set and is completely cured only after six months to one year, depending on conditions. During the first day or so after sealing the panel, excess cement will ooze out along the edges of the lead, so you should reclean the glass the day after sealing and before installing the panel. I like to wait at least one week before installing a window to be sure the cement has set well and will not ooze.

For some jobs using particularly irregular glass or multiple layers of glass, it is better to use a much thicker mixture of cement and apply it with a putty knife. When working with multiple layers of glass, thin putty will run through and

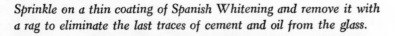

Sprinkle on a thin coating of Spanish Whitening and remove it with a rag to eliminate the last traces of cement and oil from the glass.

mark the glass surfaces sealed off by the second layer of glass, so thick cement must always be used.

After the cement has been applied and has thoroughly dried, the panel is ready for installation. After a panel has been installed, the glass should not be cleaned by any method for at least one year, because the pressure applied in wiping the glass will disrupt the seal and may cause a panel to loosen or leak. I usually recommend that a panel never be given any form of cleaning other than a simple dusting with a soft brush. For pieces in which the weathertight seal is not necessary, you may clean the lead with coarse steel wool and the glass with steel wool and a soft rag. Liquid cleaners are not recommended and rarely necessary.

REINFORCING AND INSTALLING

In a properly designed and executed small panel, no additional strengthening is needed and the panel may be installed much as an ordinary window. Although the method of installation is the same, the greater thickness of a leaded glass panel requires that the sash or door to receive it be specially made to accommodate the heavier piece. A typical panel installation is contrasted with the usual installation of an ordinary windowpane.

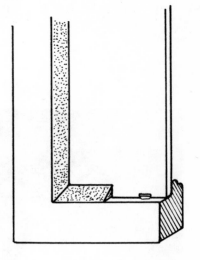

If you are making a panel to fit an old door or window, you can build the panel to fit the space. If you are building a panel to fit a new door or window, however, and the panel is to be installed at the job site, you should wait until the door or sash is finished and measure it before the panel is assembled. The amount of error accepted in some modern millwork is greater than that allowed in art-glass work, and it is not unusual to arrive at an installation to find the hole for the panel is too large or too small. An opening that is too large can usually be reduced to fit by using wooden or metal sash strips to adapt the opening to the panel. A panel that is larger than the opening, however, must be trimmed to fit. Panels edged with U-channel lead usually cannot be trimmed more than $\frac{1}{16}$ inch on any edge. Panels edged with I-type lead, however, may be trimmed as much as $\frac{3}{16}$ inch (the depth of the channel).

Panels to be installed in steel sash or in masonry walls are installed somewhat differently, but principles are the same. Those of you who wish to make such an installation should consult a professional glazier, preferably one with experience in art-glass work, before beginning your panel.

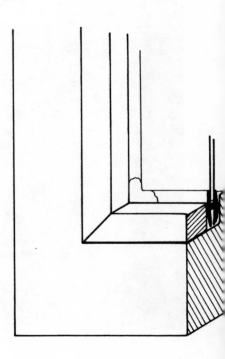

Large panels are best constructed and installed in sections. The design of such panels is done so as to allow the panel to be assembled with minimum time and danger. Some of the design considerations in this type of work will be discussed in the next chapter, but it is necessary to know something of the way such panels are installed before you can intelligently design large panels. A large panel such as the one shown in color opposite page 33 and in the diagram on page 70 is built up of rectangular pieces of glass involving only straight cutting of glass and lead. Notice in the drawing that

Use for painting

Ordinary windowpanes are held in place with glaziers' points and weather sealed with a layer of putty. An art-glass panel requires a heavier sash and must be held by wood or metal strips. It is usually set into a bed of putty to form the weather seal around the edges of the panel.

Leaded window with reinforcing bar. There is no way to hide a bar in such a window.

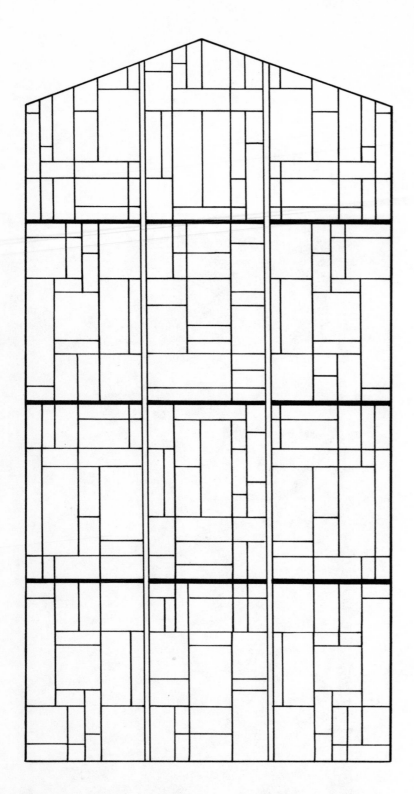

Window designed for Tharp-Sontheimer Funeral Home Chapel,
New Orleans, Louisiana.

the panel consists of twelve smaller panels, each of which was constructed and transported separately to the job site. The small panels may be assembled by installing each independently, or they may be stacked on top of each other joined by an aluminum or zinc I-channel designed for the purpose. In either case, the small panels are strong enough that no additional support or reinforcement is required, and the clean lines of the assembled panel are not broken by reinforcing bars.

In many other types of large panels, particularly tall narrow church windows or door panels, some additional support is necessary. Leaded glass must be supported in two directions: against inward and outward forces of wind and air-pressure changes, and against the downward force of the

Small panels may be combined into large windows by stacking with special channel to connect them.

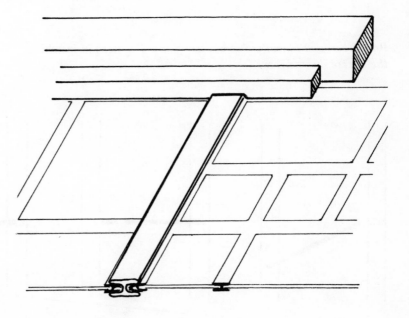

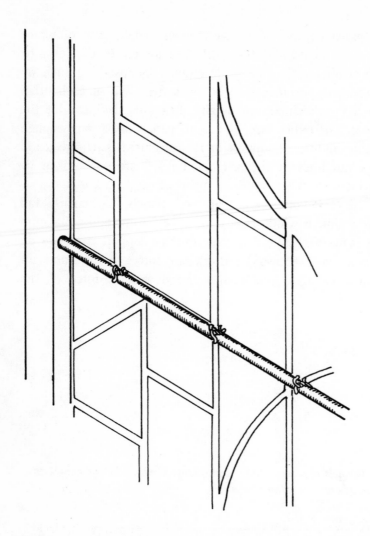

Round bar used to reinforce a window panel. The steps in installing the bar are shown below.

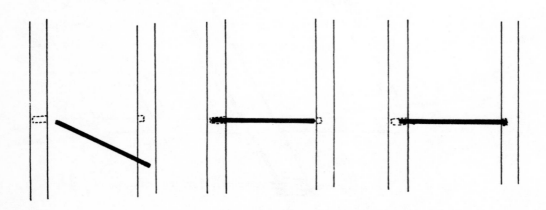

weight of the glass and the lead. Some protection against wind force and against projectiles is afforded by a second clear storm sash, often of wire-reinforced glass, installed on the outer side of the window, with at least two inches between the outer and inner windows. This sort of protection is of no use against a brick or rock, and many public places with valuable windows have added a stout steel grate or wire mesh on the outside of the storm sash. Unfortunately, grates and wire mesh cause shadows on the glass visible on the inside which may detract from the window. There is no way I know of to adequately protect a leaded window without detracting from its appearance except for tempered glass, which is usually more expensive than the leaded window and will not withstand repeated missiles.

The types of reinforcement and protection of a leaded window just mentioned do not provide reinforcement against the tendency of a heavy window to sag with time. Reinforcing bars have been and remain the best method of supporting a long window. They are of two types—round and flat. The round bar is the type used most often in older windows and is still much used today. The bar is installed after the panel has been placed in the sash by securing the bar to the sash or window casing so it lies flush against the lead of the window. It is further secured to the window by copper wire ties previously soldered to the lead. The simplest form of installation is in a wooden sash where two holes are drilled in the sash, one side deeper than the other, and the bar placed as shown in the diagram by inserting one end in the deep hole and then the other in the shallow hole.

Flat bar is usually wider than the diameter of round bar, and when it is soldered to the lead, is stronger than round bar. In windows where a section of the leaded glass is movable, the flat bar is often used to support the sections of the window adjacent to the movable part of the window. Other types of bars are available in many shapes—such as U-channel, T-section, or angle iron—with each type having particular uses.

There is, by the way, no right or wrong side to a leaded panel. I usually install a panel with the smooth side out, since dirt and dust will tend to collect on the rough side and there is presumably less dirt inside. If the wires for the reinforcing bar have already been soldered on, the choice has been made, for the bar is always inside.

THOUGHTS ON DESIGN

The person designing an art-glass panel must be aware of all the limitations of the methods of art-glass construction. Usually the master art-glass craftsman will work out the design for a panel together with the architect or owner of the building for which the panel is intended. The original idea may be a painting or drawing to be translated into glass, or the glass worker may be given a free hand to design a panel to fit a certain space. In either case, the glass worker will first make a scale drawing of the proposed panel and color it with paint or colored pencils to show the customer what the intended effect is. During this phase, the designer must always bear in mind the size limitations and structural characteristics of the materials to be used together with the skill of the man who will execute the design and come up with a design that is pleasing and appropriate to the setting within the cost limitations of the job. Upon approval of the scale drawing, the panel is drawn up full size, usually in sections, and the panel is constructed, taken to the site, and installed.

Most of you will be designing, executing, and installing your own panels, and you must expect that there will be many mistakes along the way. It takes years for a glass worker to become a master, and those years are filled with workbench experience which is gained in no other way. Those of you who are beginning to work with art glass are encouraged to keep your projects small and to avoid, at least for a time, any panels that are to be installed in a door or a sash. The best beginning projects are those involving only straight cuts and should be no larger than two feet in greatest dimension until you have learned to handle larger panels. Resist for the present the temptation to use complex designs with many curves; you will find them less frustrating and costly if you wait. Avoid using junk glass you may have picked up somewhere, such as old window glass or broken bottles, no matter how artistic you may feel. Such glass is very difficult to work with and will not hold up as well as modern art glass. It is best used by such techniques as epoxy embedding to be mentioned later.

Here are designs for several simple panels that involve only straight cuts and make ideal beginner projects. Such

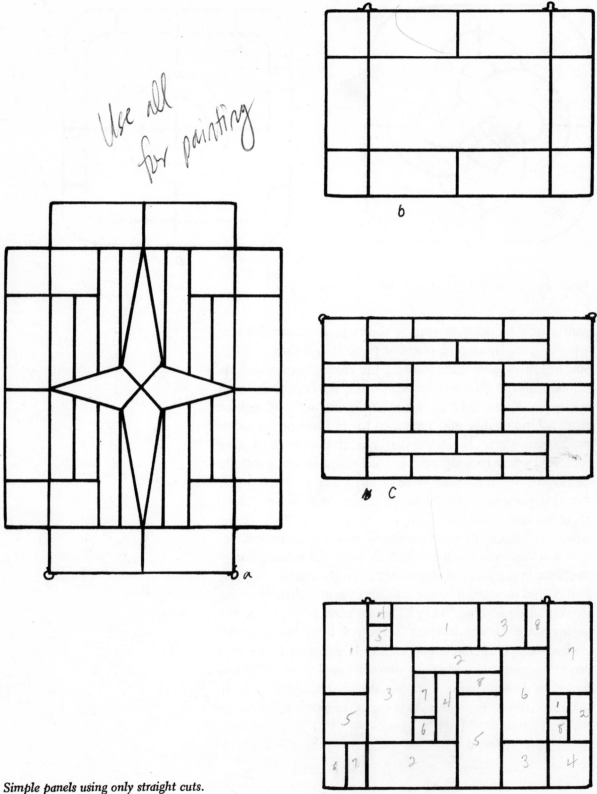

Use all for painting

Simple panels using only straight cuts.

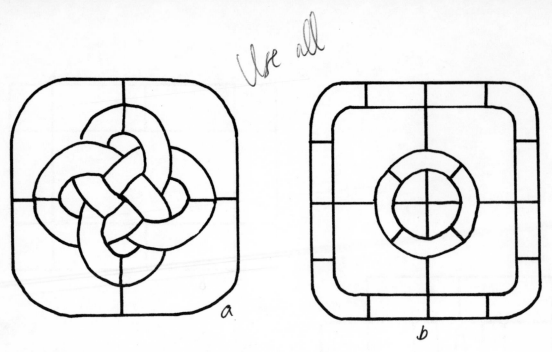

Use all

a

b

Panels with inside and compound (French) curves.

panels may be made in various sizes and in many different types of glass. By keeping your first projects as simple as these, you will spend your time learning the characteristics and appearance of the glass and, hopefully, not get bogged down in technique. Panels such as these may be framed and lighted from behind or they may be suspended in front of a window as decorative accents. In the diagrams of the panels, I have indicated where hanging wires are to be attached to panels to be suspended. In hanging these or any other panels, remember that the panels should be supported from points where there are leads running through from top to bottom of the panel. An incorrectly hung panel will gradually pull apart.

The first curves you cut should be gradual outside curves as shown in the practice panels. After you have mastered these curves, you may begin to use inside curves and sharper curves in your designs. The "LOVE" panel used to illustrate the earlier stages in construction is really a fairly sophisticated design, despite its simple appearance. If you wish to attempt something similar, you could make a panel with initials, a name, or a monogram. A simple block-letter alphabet is diagramed for you to follow. As you can see, cutting the pieces for such letters would not be easy.

I have included some pictures of more elaborate panels

Example a

Use
all

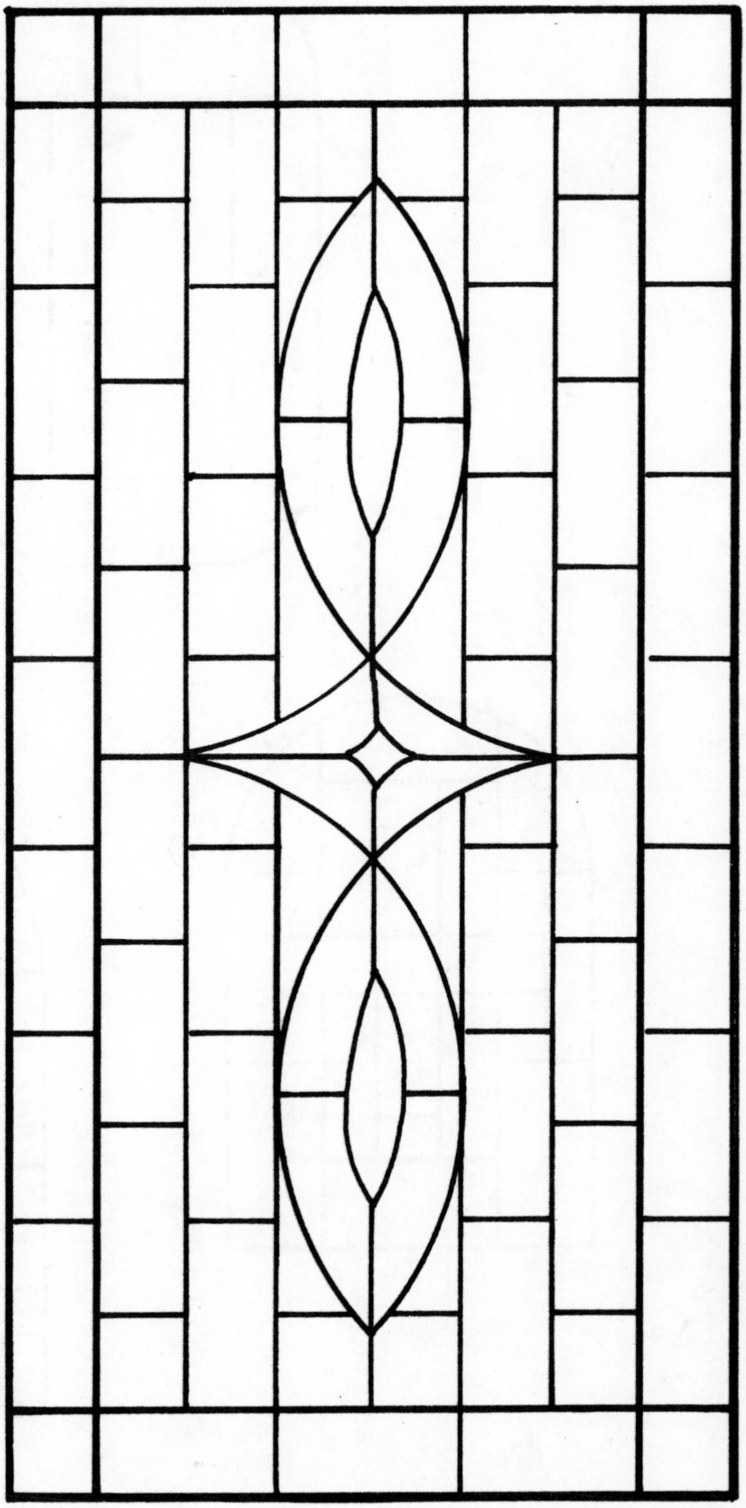

77

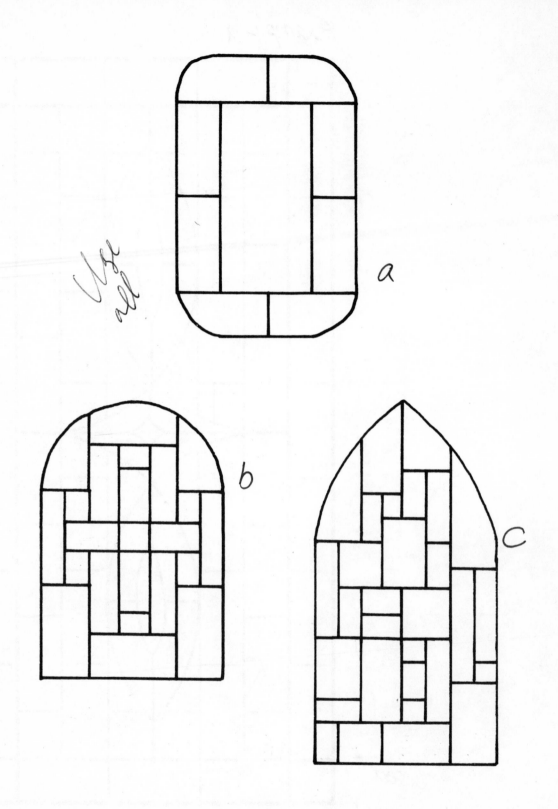

Use
all

a

b

c

Simple panels with outside curves.

ABCDE
FGHIJK
LMNOP
QRSTU
VWXYZ

used in stained glass writing

Block-letter alphabet designed for ease of cutting.

illustrating the traditional and the modern styles in art-glass design. There is no right and wrong in design, as long as the design is structurally sound and the panel well made. With experience, you will learn your own particular limitations of technique and will design within the scope of your ability to carry out the design.

In recent years, the use of glass in works of art or architecture has increased, and many people have begun to explore new ways in which to use glass. For example, large chunks of glass have been used to build walls or have been embedded in walls. These glass chunks are usually purchased from glass manufacturers and are made from the glass formed along the outside rim of large mixing tanks in which the molten glass is compounded. This type of glass has many swirled layers and many faults in it and is usually in irregular chunks produced when the tanks are cleaned by breaking the glass out with sledge hammers. Such glass is not useful in leaded panels because of its thickness and irregularity, so it is often embedded directly into a masonry wall or into a plastic-resin panel, which is then installed much as a window. The problems with the use of this type of glass arise from the fact that glass has a different expansion and contraction rate than masonry, metal, or wood. This fact is the main reason why glass is nearly always installed in a bed of flexible material, such as putty or vinyl plastic. The flexible mounting accommodates the different expansion and contraction of the glass and the sash as the temperature changes and in addition provides a cushion against sudden gusts of wind or changes in pressure. Glass embedded directly in masonry lacks this protection and will usually either work loose or crack with time. The plastic resin used to embed glass, as in the so-called "epoxy windows" may or may not have an expansion and contraction rate the same as the glass. If it doesn't, the glass will work loose or the plastic will crack in time. If you want to try using glass in epoxy resin or polyester resin, remember that we just don't know how long such panels will hold up.

As a craftsman, I like to feel that my work will survive for several lifetimes, so I work almost exclusively with leaded glass panels. From time to time, someone may wish another sort of decorative glass, such as an epoxy window, and in those cases I make sure that the customer understands that there is no way of predicting the lifetime of the finished piece.

Leaded glass panels using clear glass. Above and page 82.

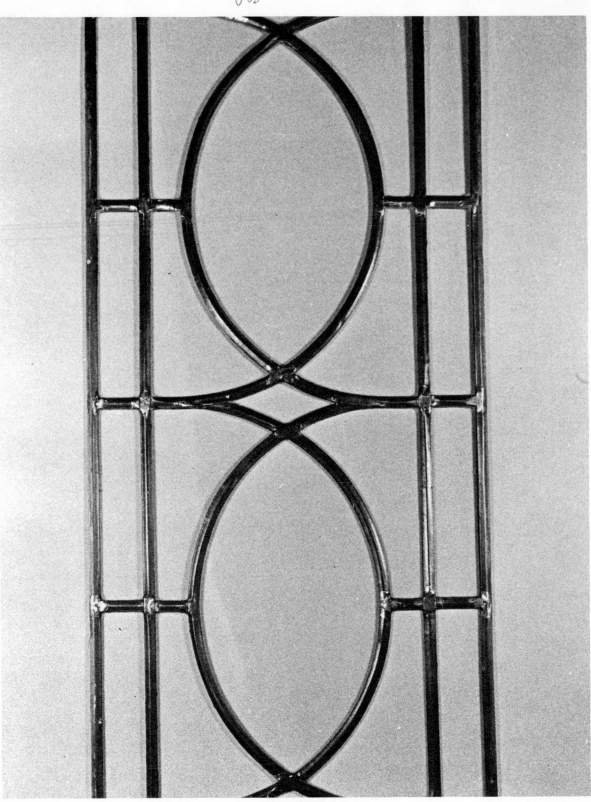

Example image

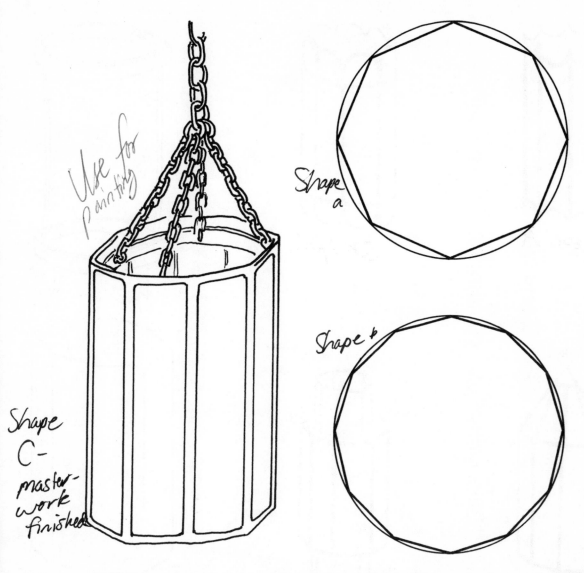

Use for painting

Shape a

Shape b

Shape C— master- work finished

Simple cylindrical lamp

An eight-sided lamp will have sharper angles than a twelve-sided one. The glass will be more likely to separate from the lead in the lamp with sharper angles.

After some experience with flat panels, you may want to try three dimensional construction. The simplest project is a cylindrical lamp as shown here. When designing such a lamp, you must remember that the narrower the strips of glass and the more sides, the nearer the lamp comes to a true circle and the better the fit of the glass and the lead. If the angles to be made are too acute, the glass will not fit in the channel properly and will pop out in time. There is special zinc channel

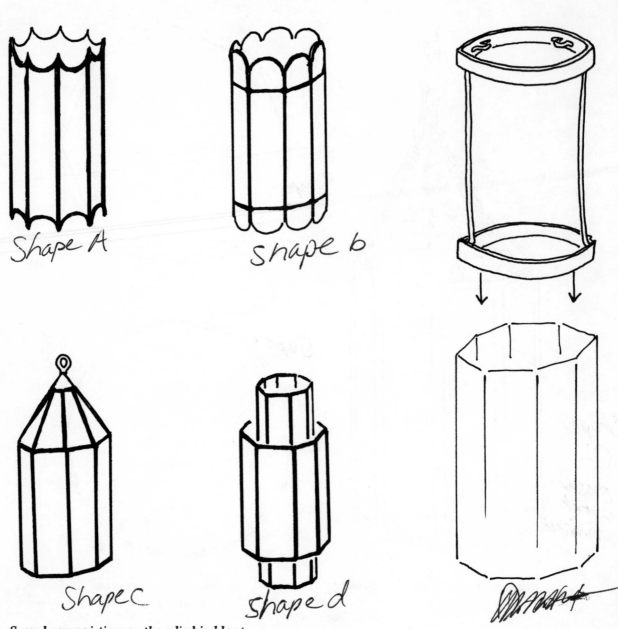

Shape A

shape b

Shape c

shape d

Several easy variations on the cylindrical lamp.

The inner skeleton of the lamp should support the lamp at top and bottom. The frame can be bent from brass welding rod and soldered to the lead of the lamp.

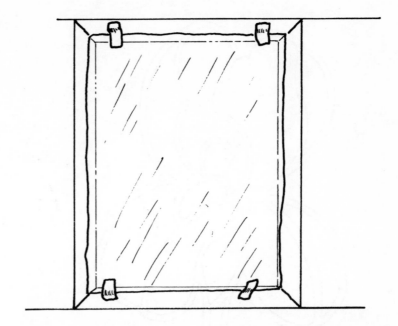

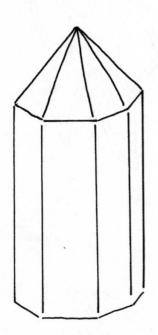

In many lamps, the glass can be held by small brass or copper clips.

A standing lamp needs support only at the bottom.

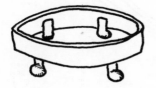

available for 90-, 60-, 45-, and 30-degree joints in glass, but this channel is expensive and hard to find. Here are several variations on this type of lamp. After the lamp has been leaded, it is necessary that it be properly suspended, or the lead will gradually deform and separate from the glass. The best suspension system is a collar around the bottom and top rims which is fastened to the lead with copper wire and solder and forms attachment for a chain if the lamp is to hang. If the lamp is to stand on a base, you may wish to make a bottom with feet, as shown. As you experiment with lamps many ideas will occur to you. If you wish to use art glass in a lamp made of sheet metal, such as copper or tin, you will probably find the glass is secured by small metal tabs, as shown, instead of being mounted in lead channel. Such glass may be removed and replaced by bending the tabs. Cement or putty is not usually used in such installations.

The lamps shown in the color pictures following page 64 are made using glass which has been bent for the purpose. The art of bending glass for such lamps has been nearly lost for many years, but with the recent interest in "Tiffany" style lamps, we have begun to experiment with bending glass in order to repair or reproduce the older lamps. The equipment and supplies required for this sort of work places it far beyond the scope of an introductory book, however.

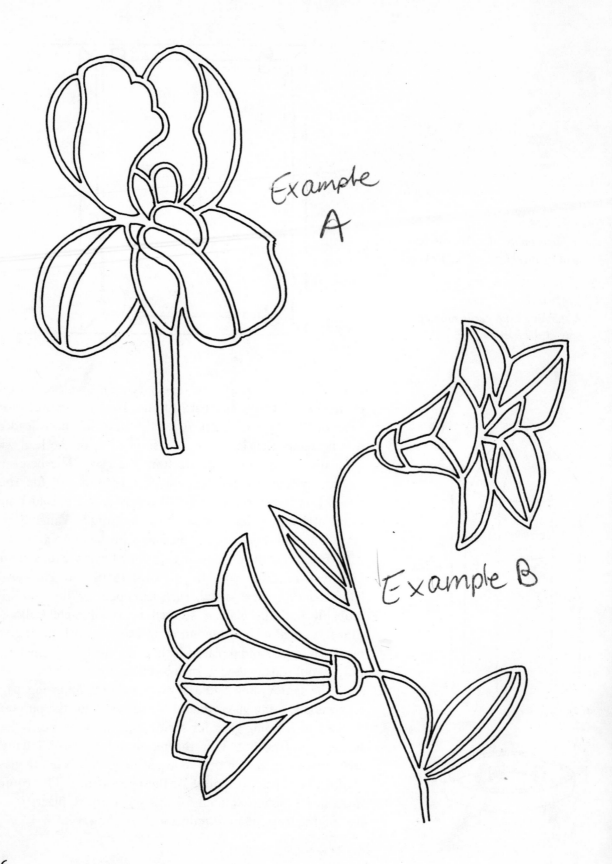

Example
A

Example B

Use all

Example
C

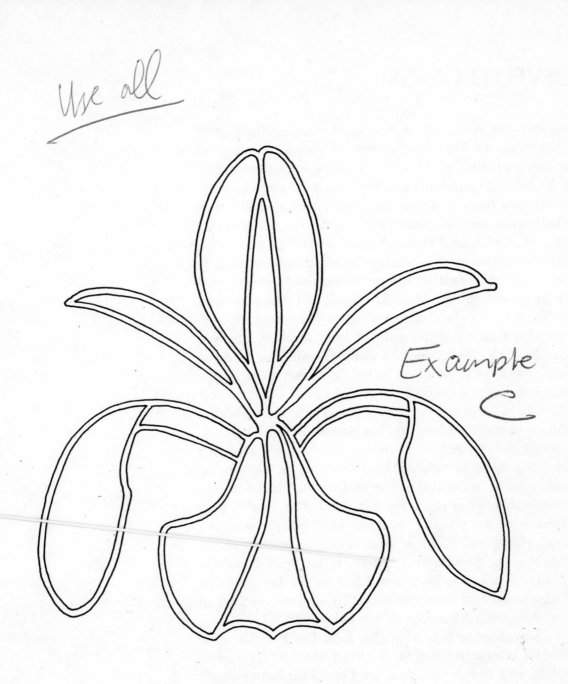

Several flower patterns for the advanced worker.

BEVELED GLASS

Beveled-glass panels are constructed of many small pieces of plate glass each with all edges beveled assembled in a panel to create a multifaceted pattern. The beveled surfaces reflect light and act as prisms so that a panel used in a door, transom, or window becomes a sparkling, many-colored design constantly changing appearance as the light changes during the day. At night, lighted from behind, a beveled glass panel becomes a crystal jewel delighting the passer-by. This type of work was very popular in the last century and the early part of the present century. Many fine panels still remain in older buildings in cities such as New Orleans. Because of the high cost of materials and the hours of labor involved, however, glass beveling is something of a vanished craft. The following brief discussion is presented in the hope that some of you may wish to revive the craft.

The patterns used in beveled panels may be identical or similar to those used in art-glass panels. Usually, however, panels to be executed in beveled glass are designed especially for the purpose because certain limitations in the beveling technique, or in the skill of the worker, must be taken into consideration when laying out the panel. The beveled glass panel must be designed to avoid large pieces, extremely small pieces, and shapes with acute angles, because of the difficulties in beveling such pieces. If the man doing the beveling is a master craftsman, however, the limitations of design are not as severe although the expense involved in time-consuming difficult bevels may not be justified.

A single pane of beveled glass looks like this. The glass used for beveling is either ¼- or ⅜-inch plate. Older workers usually used ⅜-inch plate glass, but I prefer the lighter weight ¼-inch glass. In the beveling process, the edgemost ½ inch

In beveled glass work, each piece is tapered to ⅛-inch thickness along each edge.

is ground off at an angle and then polished to a smooth transparent surface. In thicker glass, the angle produced will be steeper than that made when the thinner glass is used, but the visual effect in a completed panel will be the same.

Regardless of the thickness of the glass used, the beveling process is the same. There are two steps: Grinding, in which the edge of the glass is mechanically abraded away to make the desired bevel, and polishing, in which the ground opaque surface is finely polished until it is as smooth and transparent as the original surface of the glass.

There is no particular "right" way to bevel glass. The techniques I use were learned through years of trial-and-error work and are largely based on the equipment I use, which was acquired from a predecessor in the glass business. I suspect my methods are as antiquated as my equipment, so I'll make no specific recommendations, which may only mislead the beginner. Instead, I would like to make some general suggestions about how an interested person could approach learning the technique and acquiring the tools and skills required.

Probably the best way to start beveling glass is to find out what abrasive wheels and compounds are available locally or by mail. Try a few small wheels and various grits on some scrap plate glass until you find a combination suitable for grinding and one for polishing. As you experiment, remember that the greatest problem will be the heating which occurs in any grinding or polishing process. Work slowly, with the wheels revolving at low speeds and with constant addition of water or oil to keep the wheel and the glass cool. Overheating the glass will cause it to chip or crack. After you have experimented with beveling on a small scale, you will be better able to decide whether or not you want to undertake the rather large expense of the equipment required for beveling on a large scale.

For a medium-sized beveling operation, you'll need about 100 square feet of shop space for the machinery and supplies. Layout and assembly of the panels can be done in the assembly area of an ordinary shop, as the process is about the same.

You will need two or more large electric motors, assorted drive shafts, pulleys, and belts as well as heavy-duty dust-proof bearing assemblies for the large wheels. For large work, you should have at least two large wheels (12 to 36 inch

Because only the last ½ inch of the glass is beveled, thicker glass will have a steeper angle than a thinner glass.

Careless beveling of even a simple piece will result in misalignment
of the bevels at the corners.

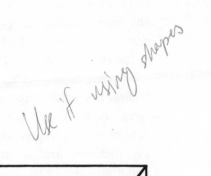

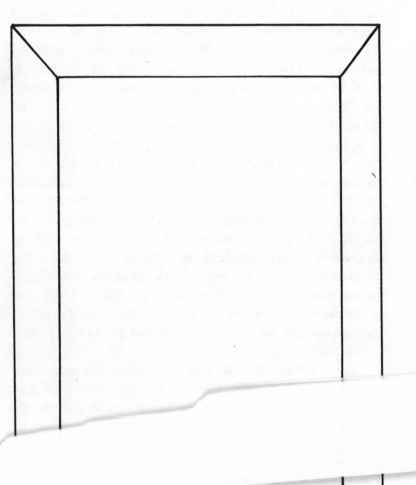

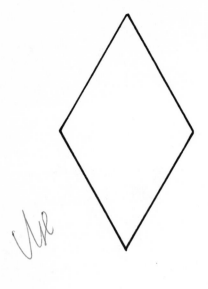

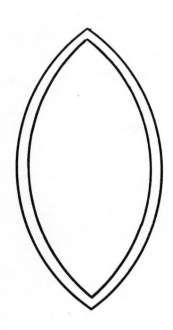

diameter) run horizontally like a record player turntable mounted at table-top height to provide large surfaces for beveling. One wheel will be for grinding; the second for polishing. Do not attempt to use the same wheel for both operations, as it is impossible to completely clean the abrasive compounds from a wheel, and residual fine grit will clog a grinding wheel, while residual coarse grit will cause scratching if left on the polishing wheel. You should also have a good assortment of smaller wheels which may be run vertically and used for beveling small or curved pieces.

If you haven't been discouraged by the information presented so far, you might find a few comments on technique helpful. Beveling a simple square or rectangular piece of glass presents no particular difficulty, other than the need to produce uniform bevels. When beveling a piece with an acute angle, however, the narrow part of the glass will often break with the heating that occurs in the grinding and polishing processes. Curved pieces are particularly difficult to master and are best avoided in designs, unless the beveler is exceptionally skilled. Small circles, especially those that are to be faceted (jewels), are nearly impossible. Even though I've been beveling glass for a number of years, I still occasionally break a piece, usually in the final polishing stage when the edge is finest and most fragile. I figure that it takes between a half to one hour to bevel each piece in the average panel.

The panels may be assembled with lead or zinc cames. Zinc is most definitely preferred because its greater strength is required to support the weight of the plate glass. The methods of assembly and reinforcing the panel are as already described.

As you may have concluded, I do not expect many of you will be beveling glass in the near future, but as a practitioner of this nearly extinct craft, I wanted to take this opportunity to perhaps introduce it to a wider audience. Any of you wishing to learn more about glass beveling or art glass in general is welcome to visit my studio in New Orleans.

Pieces with acute angles are more difficult to bevel. Top.

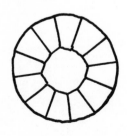

Curves, circles, and faceted "jewels" are most difficult to bevel.

GLOSSARY

ABRASION. Any mechanical grinding or polishing process, such as those used in surface finishing of plate glass or in edge beveling of glass.

ART GLASS. In general, any glass used for its beauty rather than strictly for utilitarian purposes. Used generally to refer to colored glass assembled into panels, lamps, or the like.

BEAD. A strip of molding, usually wood or metal, used in the installation of windows or leaded panels.

BLEMISH. Any fault in a piece of glass. In art glass, blemishes may be deliberately created to enhance the artistic appearance of the glass.

BUTT JOINT. A joint, usually a right angle, in which the two pieces joined simply lie next to each other, rather than being overlapped or notched.

together in an art g....

CASEMENT WINDOW. A window with hinges on the vertical side or sides as contrasted to the more conventional sash in which the window opens by sliding up or down in vertical troughs.

CAULK. To seal a narrow opening or space with special soft material to weather seal a building, especially around doors and windows. Unlike the new plastic putties, caulking compounds usually harden with exposure to the elements, so are not used for installing or weather sealing glass.

CHAMFER. A beveled edge.

CORROSION. Chemical destruction of a substance, as in acid etching of glass.

CULLET. Cutoffs and scrap pieces of glass.

DOUBLE GLAZING. The setting of two individual panes of glass in two single frames or one double frame joined and sealed to make a single unit with two layers of glass enclosing an air space. Although used primarily to make insulated windows, double glazing was formerly done in art-glass work when it was necessary to use more than one piece of glass to create the desired color or texture in a leaded glass panel.

FLAKING. The small chips of glass produced along the score mark when excessive pressure is applied with the cutting wheel.

FLASHED GLASS. Colored glass produced by fusing a layer of colored glass to a layer of clear glass. When the colored glass is etched or sandblasted away, the treated areas will appear clear against a colored background.

FLUX. A substance used in soldering to assist the solder in flowing and forming a strong joint between the pieces being soldered.

GLASS. An amorphous compound of fused silica sand, soda lime, and other materials such as borates and phosphates with the chemical properties of a supercooled liquid. Glass is usually transparent, but may be treated during manufacture to produce translucent or semiopaque material of many different colors and textures.

GLAZING. The installing of glass in window frames, doors, and other openings.

LIGHT. Any of the pieces of glass in a window; a general term meaning any leaded panel containing transparent glass. Also, any piece of transparent or translucent flat glass.

MITER. A type of joint in which the joined pieces are each cut at an angle that is half of the angle of the joint; in a ninety-degree miter joint, each piece is cut at a forty-five-degree angle.

MULLION. The vertical division between two adjacent windows.

MUNTIN. The horizontal bar separating two windowpanes or lights.

PLATE GLASS. Flat drawn sheet glass that has been surface ground and polished to remove all surface irregularities and visual distortions. Plate glass comes in many thicknesses and is available in several special types such as heat-absorbent and tempered plate.

PUTTY. A compound of weatherproof cements and oils used in setting glass to provide a cushion and weather seal between the sash and the glass. Originally powdered chalk and linseed oil, modern putty is made of various plastics and will not harden with age, so it continues to form a cushion for the glass.

SASH. The wooden or metal framework that holds the glass in a window.

SEED. A small air bubble within a piece of glass. In art glass, seeds are not considered faults but are regarded as enhancing the appearance of the glass.

SILL. The horizontal framing member at the bottom of a window or door.

SOLDER. A metal alloy, commonly of lead and tin, melted to form a joint between two pieces of metal.

SPALL. A chip on the edge of a piece of glass.

STAINED GLASS. Art glass that has been painted with special pigment and kiln-fired to fuse the pigment with the glass. Incorrectly used by the layman to refer to any colored glass.

STORM WINDOW or STORM SASH. An extra window fitted outside the regular window to provide weather protection, usually removable.

TEMPLATE. A pattern used in cutting glass.

TRANSOM. A small window over a door or another window, usually providing ventilation when the door or main window is closed.

WHEEL. The glazier's term for the steel-wheeled glass cutter.

LIST OF SUPPLIERS

GLASS
National Mail Order Houses with Art Glass in Stock

Whittemore-Durgin Glass Company
Box 2065
Hanover, Mass. 02339

American Handicrafts Company
The Tandy Corporation
8117 Highway 80 West
Fort Worth, Tex. 76116

In New York
S. A. Bendheim Company
122 Hudson Street
New York, N.Y., 10013

In New Orleans
Claude Lips
2766 Gladiolus Street
New Orleans, La. 70122

TOOLS

Somer and Maca Company
5501 West Ogden Avenue
Chicago, Ill. 60650

Whittemore-Durgin Company
Box 2065
Hanover, Mass. 02339